WHAT'S HAPPENING TO OUR TV

SAMIA RAHMAN

Copyright

What's Happening to Our TV

Copyright © 2016 by Samia Rahman
www.samiarahman.com

All rights reserved.

Book design by Samia Rahman
Cover art by Reo / al.sal.sabil.reo@gmail.com

Samia Rahman

Printed in the United States of America by CreateSpace (an Amazon company)

First Printing: October 2016

ISBN: 1539088383

ISBN-13: 978-1539088387

———— • ————

"Nobody ever figures out what life is all about,
and it doesn't matter. Explore the world. Nearly
everything is really interesting if you go into it
deeply enough. Work as hard and as much as
you want to on the things you like to do the
best. Don't think about what you want to be,
but what you want to do. "

-RICHARD FEYNMAN-

CONTENTS

PREFACE

From my childhood, mass media have been a topic of interest for me. Not because of being involved in the media industry and teaching in the journalism field for a long time, but mass media is my passion- for facing new challenges every day.

The rapid dynamic shift of global mass media is creating global revolution while at the same time we observe frustrations of the audiences in Bangladesh about the local media and being a media professional, I also need to take this liability.

This was the fundamental concern that motivated me to write this book.

My previous published books also focused on the issues of mass media. But since they were written in the Bengali language, the readers outside Bangladesh were not able to understand the emptiness, scopes and instability in Bangladeshi media to raise any constructive discussion or criticism.

There is no doubt that it is our duty to figure out the possibilities of our own media as it is not possible to deny the perspective of Bangladesh by only imitating the global media world. But for the population of 160 million, 28 TV channels in Bangladesh are still reflecting a small mass media market. On the other hand, the one-sided cultural invasion of neighboring countries is more upsetting due to the commercial bureaucracy. Regardless of all these problems, the TV channels in Bangladesh still have great potentials. It is now the right time to start analyzing our mass media from the perspective of audiences for its success.

When we view, listen or read from mass media then we start subconsciously acting as a critic. Being able to answer the criticism of the audiences can thus truly revolutionize the mass media. I am ready to accept any critic about this book since I have always been on the role of a critic. Especially if this book can initiate complex thinking for the readers, if the content seems prudent for the TV audiences for meeting their demands and meet the need to handle different crisis and emptiness with the TV for different mass media owners and entrepreneurs for creating a potential situation in Bangladesh mass media, then my attempt will be successful.

It can be questionable where are the gaps with all these existing medias, freedom and programs, where are the crisis? This book tried to answer these questions. I have tried to draw a line in this book, using my sixteen years practical work experience in mass media together with my theoretical academic knowledge and teaching experiences.

ACKNOWLEDGEMENTS

This book became a reality with the kind support and help of many individuals. I would like to extend my sincere thanks to all of them. First of all, I would like to express my gratefulness to the vice chancellor of University of Dhaka, Dr. Arefin Siddique, who has always helped and co-operated me at work, in teaching and research.

I want to express my love and respect to the former news editor of Bangladesh Television, Fuad Hasan, my brother-in-law, who was my first inspiration towards the love of television. My thanks, appreciations, and love goes to my children, Tirtho and Ayushman who have continuously been my inspiration in life and my greatest achievements ever. For them, I am living and loving my life and work. I express my gratitude to my father Quazi Mahamudur Rahman and my mother Dilruba Rahman for continually being supportive and staying by my side under any circumstances. My father being the former director (program) of Radio Bangladesh actually, has propagated the seed of interest for mass media in me.

I want to express my love to Adrita Tasnim, my niece, studying Broadcast Journalism at the University of North Texas, whom I believe have inspired to get into media studies.

I want to express my thanks to many friends and colleagues, owners and management individuals from the Bangladesh media world, particularly with those who I have experience working with.

Finally, I would like to thank numerous mass media readers, listeners and audiences who have always been my inspiration and center of all success.

SAMIA RAHMAN

" Learn from yesterday, live for today, hope for tomorrow. The important thing is not to stop questioning. "

-Albert Einstein-

———— ♦ ————

Many of the rich and successful people in the world are not necessarily well educated, very talented or even good looking. They became successful because they wanted to be.

Our high school friends who were top in the class are not always the one who prospered in their life than their other peers.

This is why, while addressing these opinions, Paul Arden chose the title of his bestselling book to be 'It's not how good you are, it's how good you want to be'[1]. Similarly, Henry Petroski in his book 'Success through Failure: The paradox of design' stated, 'desire, not necessity, is the mother of invention'[2]. 'What's Happening to Our TV' is a book transcribed with a determination not only to show what are the contemporary electronic media trends in Bangladesh but to illustrate what can be done beyond those drifts and in what way they can be accomplished.

As a student of mass communication and journalism, I used to ask myself about the apprehensions related to our TV industry, what is going on with it and where is it heading towards.

Discussions with my academic friends and the relatives then made one thing clear for me- they did not seem to bother much about it.

During my early professional career in academia and electronic media, I still had the quest of discovering the answer to this question. This time, I was conferring with my students, academic colleagues and skilled media professionals about the eminence and image of electronic media in Bangladesh. Unfortunately, I had to be disappointed by their reaction this time too.

While many of them had no traces about what was going on, the saddest part was that a lot of them thought there was zero going on in our electronic media expansion. It seemed to me, even though we professionals took an interest on this issue and students were concerned to explore the facts regarding this, we simply did not even know where to turn or start.

After spending over more than a decade in professional media experience along with relevant academic research in university I was still left with a mixed up feelings while trying to find an answer to this question.

———— • ————

I gradually started realizing that there is a remarkable lack of resource and reference for exploring this issue from the perspective of Bangladesh. Because I knew what it means to be a media professional. It is like constantly being in a state of fluidity. New technologies and new ways of thinking about making content to cope up with the never ending audience demands are swiftly providing and pushing us the media professionals, to drastically rethink what we are actually doing. In this respect, I could not find literature concerning the explorative and extrapolative analysis of electronic media in Bangladesh to image the future.

I then stopped my effort to know the answer and instead planned to do something about it, because it is always exciting to solve a problem than to identify the answer directly. That incentive was the principal foundation that made me start writing a book you are reading today.

What do professionals want to know about the electronic media in Bangladesh? While searching for an answer to this question, specialized individuals interested in media do not want to know what program or talk show is popular in Bangladesh TV channels or how to use the electronic media from a technological perspective. What the experts want to know is what is happening with the TV industry in Bangladesh?

Specifically, they want to know where it is heading, what new business ideas we can generate to improve productivity and to find updated research materials for improving their expertise. From beginner media, mass communication or journalism students to seasoned professionals in this field interested in media development in Bangladesh, ask same questions.

Are there any glitches in present-day electronic media in Bangladesh? What are they and what needs to be done to decipher and develop them? What would happen if we do not take proper movements in time? How can new technology use affect the future of individuals as a role of an audience? What are the psychologies behind persuading audiences in a content generation? How should we act to take advantages in realizing hidden psychology of audiences in relation to content? What new ways the content generation will take its shape in the approaching future? What defines the excellence of content for Bangladesh society? How does the new media's globalization and internet trigger a social revolution? What dangers are out there for the upcoming generations for adapting such digital shifts?

How is it possible to locate new markets of electronic media and increase sell? How are these trends in electronic media going to make a difference from traditional system?

These questions have not been addressed by outdated books on electronic media or by any writer's guide since the questions are specifically focused within the context of electronic media in Bangladesh. I recognized that people interested in Bangladesh electronic media are keen for materials that can help them realizing the trends to do research about the effectiveness of improving electronic media in Bangladesh –materials that not only informs them about it but also tells them how these materials could be used for research and development. The book 'What's Happening to Our TV' is designed to answer these questions, and more.

———————— ♦ ————————

What I aim to do here is to deliver in plain English the answers to the above questions that are written from the perspective of my own experience and research. This book thus explores the interplay between present trends and beyond in the direction of the success of the electronic media business in Bangladesh and in particular, describes the important role played by modern audiences, understanding their advanced psychology for the expectation of improved content management and new marketing prospect for a digital social revolution in attaining success.

Regardless of a massive technological and new media expansion boom happened in Bangladesh, the commanding application of these phenomena is yet to be visible at hand.

One of the fundamental reasons behind it according to me is, limiting our thoughts within a certain borderline. Individuals involved in the Bangladesh media industry are afraid of asking why instead they are too busy with knowing how. I refer Simon Sinek in this respect, who in his bestseller used a scheme called "The Golden Circle" to strengthen the argument that asking "why" we do things is more important than asking "what" we do, or "how" we do[4].

According to Simon, inspired leaders and organizations think, act and communicate from the inside out regardless of the size of their industry[4]. It would be nicer if media professionals and policy makers in Bangladesh would ask themselves, why we do what we have started doing and how to bring this cause to create improved content within the context of all the technologies and market opportunities available today.

A reflection of inability in such thinking was the primary reason I never found the answers to my question.

Worthy thinking like this is thus challenging, but can solve different problems for building organization and showing the path towards a brighter future[3]. Thinking good and outside the boundary can make individuals and organizations successful and they can rule themselves[3]. By this type of thinking I believe creativity can be blossomed.

A great idea should not be allowed to be talked out by others since forcing yourself in the same old rut cannot allow you to do something new and exciting[3]. Exposing yourself to new paradigm is the most effective way to help you get out of the box.

That way, non-creative people can become creative by the support of the right environment.

So it is important to ask if we are breaking out the box to think for experiencing creative breakthroughs.

While exploring several answers to the questions presented above throughout the writing of this book, I had to do such upright thinking to break through by box of limitation in thoughts. Thus, this book is simply an example of such thinking-outside the scope of traditional beliefs concerning the electronic media topics in Bangladesh.

This book is all about giving yourself an authorization to think what you can do instead of what you are capable of doing in regard to the electronic media prospect in Bangladesh. It demonstrates you to see the highly prospective media world of Bangladesh and its potentials through the eyes of a child.

However the goal of this book should not be misunderstood to be a solution to things that are not working in Bangladesh electronic media instead it should be taken as a guide and focus on different things that needs serious attention in Bangladesh media scenarios. This book will not tell you what to do or how to do by showing any course of actions instead the goal is to offer you the cause of action.

There may be other solutions that others may think of regarding the issues of electronic media in Bangladesh. However, what is important to note here is that asking the right question is the basis of generating the right answers[4].

My attempt in this book was therefore to ask the right questions for understanding the proper cause of issues related to electronic media in Bangladesh and thereby steer towards solutions.

In every Chapter of this book you will find numerous logical, practical ideas, and principles that will enable you to tie together the massive strength of thinking outside the box, for the success of electronic media in Bangladesh where you can play the fundamental role as a student, researcher or a media professional.

I have tried to give different real life examples for the illustration of different ideas. You discover not only what to do, but, how to apply different principles and suggestions to actual situations and problems. In this respect, this is what the book will do for you; it will show you how you can implement things. As you read the Chapters committed to a specific aspect of electronic media development issue in Bangladesh, you will learn that they do not try to tell you not only what to think but also aim to clarify you how to implement what you think.

The book is divided into five Chapters. Each Chapter highlights a particular aspect of electronic media issues in Bangladesh and explains how that aspect can be affected.

Chapter 1 presents the discussions related to the modern audiences. It elaborates the distinctions between traditional and modern audience. This Chapter will discuss different strategies specifically tailored to understand audiences in Bangladesh. A goal here is to introduce a language for thinking about the role of audiences and their potentials that have evolved over the years. Strengths and characteristics of modern Bangladesh audiences will be identified and how they can be used for exploring the potential of electronic media development will be addressed.

Chapter 2 updates the topic of persuasion within the context of media content development and user. Persuasion took a different shift over time and as the audience nature is changing so is their way of getting persuaded too. The pervasive nature of persuasion is important to practice for utilizing the psychology of modern audiences for improved content creation. This Chapter will discuss different scopes, possibilities and aspects of psychology that can be used to bond between audience expectation and content generation. When and how can experts trust audience perception to be intuitive? Are there any specific patterns that can be followed?

What cognitive model can be a handy tool for the authorities dealing with these issues? I attempt to give a sense of these topics in this Chapter.

The concerns related to electronic media content contribute to the main theme of **Chapter 3** which describes the state of affairs related to the electronic media content in Bangladesh and shows how to get over with this. Why is it important for Bangladesh media professional to stress importance of content generation?

How the future business scopes can be shaped on the basis of quality content? Are there any associated risks in this process? My views on these issues along with content, design method and process by taking advantage of audience insight will also be deliberated in this Chapter.

The focus of **Chapter 4** is discussing economic extensions related to electronic media development in Bangladesh. Since we are living in a digital age and an information technology revolution has already taken place in Bangladesh, it is apparent that improve content generation would mean new business opportunities.

This Chapter will discuss the present scopes of economics in the media business, its drawbacks and remedies. The topic of digital media economics is an attention-grabbing and significant aspect of the media business that is often ignored during the planning phase of content generation.

This Chapter will highlight the context of Bangladesh and its potentials for enhancing the digital media economics for the future and will propose steps on how to adapt those features.

What could be the effective guidelines for taking expert experiences from in-house contents to a successful business scenario? What are the risks associated with it?

What should be the business strategies for the foreign audiences?

Are there any agile, cost-effective models that media professionals can use within the context of Bangladesh society to restructure their existing strategies for economic success in the media business?

Chapter 5 describes an indicated digital social revolution through the future electronic media in Bangladesh. An immense opening towards a digital revolt is extrapolated here by summarizing the different combinatorial effects of different aspects of electronic media issues in Bangladesh discussed throughout the book.

What needs to be done to prepare us for such a revolution? Why do we need to approve ourselves and be ready for such acceptance? How do we do it?

What could be the advantages and disadvantages for our future generations for such alteration?

What lessons can we learn from other cultures and countries to imply them into the growth of electronic media in Bangladesh?

Why we are not being able to take full potential of such revolution yet and how can we overcome that?

What should policymakers do in these respects and what are the roles of politics regarding these in Bangladesh?

I will deliberate these topics briefly in Chapter 5.

A concluding Chapter explores, the holistic question of what exactly is happening to our TV in Bangladesh and what trends have we discovered beyond traditional electronic media as it is now? This section in return refers us back to shape the thoughts of the audiences which would signpost an iterative process of electronic media research and development for Bangladesh.

There are, of course, numerous other factors besides audiences, their psychologies, content and new business scopes in a digital social uprising focused Bangladesh, which the reader may call to mind that affects electronic media development- including the ethical, political and historical- but it is not likely for any solitary book to say the whole thing.

I personally am indeed gratified of this book and the advice left in it. I want the readers to get a road map for building an improved capacity to breed and utilize fresh ideas in media development in Bangladesh. Like in Scott Belsky's bestseller *"Making Ideas Happen"*[5], people are driven by different great interest and ideas to follow them were in my mind while I was writing this book.

I hope that this book gives you the confidence to look into the issues of electronic media in Bangladesh from an innovative perspective; regardless of your background and that the essence of this book will encourage you in exploring those viewpoints entirely.

But then again, there is a chance that you may not like this book and as a matter of fact, you may hate it. If the book seems puzzling, if it scares and discourages you, then be sure to believe that you do not have what it takes to be the future leader of the media industry in Bangladesh. Since courage is the fundamental virtue what the prospective leaders ought to inaugurate them upon. Yet, given that, there is nothing wrong just to be an amateur audience.

CHAPTER

THE NEW AUDIENCES

" God is a comedian playing to an audience too afraid to laugh "

-Voltaire-

Understanding the users is the key to any effective research. It is no surprise that analyzing audience has been one of the fundamental interests for media professional in determining the success of diverse electronic media contents.

After all it is the appetite of audiences that structure the foundation of electronic media and its success. Knowing more about the audiences has created diverse new essential elements in communication theories while at the same time it helps us understand the role of electronic media on different social impacts[1]. In the quest of learning about new media, we ask frequently what actually are "new"[1] in the new media paradigm?

But what we often overlook is the way new media has made an impact on shaping the audience and their characteristics. Similarly, it is important to ask what, actually, do we mean by new media? Yesterday's new media is changing rapidly with the rapid movement of technology that is creating audiences who are continuously adapting themselves to be included in the process of their personal development which in the long run contributes towards media development. This phenomenon is particularly interesting from the perspective of Bangladesh.

Present audiences - their way of thinking, expectation, demand and analyzing ability are nothing but equally parallel to any developed country's concerned audiences due to the globalization and massive enclosure of new technologies and the information superhighway.

Therefore, while considering the competence of current audiences in Bangladesh we need to think differently- even comparing from the era of first private TV channel in Bangladesh there was a huge difference on how audience then and now are thinking, learning and acting. Audience demand has increased and evolved over these time periods in Bangladesh.

———— • ————

To explore these demands, it is important to realize that the audiences are getting new contents through the broadcast of new media. What actually are those new contents mean to the audiences? Majority researchers studying audience and their perception in Bangladesh often are focusing on an unrepresentative group of the population and trying to find out issues like technology that do not really represent the whole mass population of Bangladesh.

Researchers do understand the need for including different subjects to analyze audiences, but it is merely studied rather discussed only. Therefore, what new media is all about for western world should not be perceived to be similar for Bangladesh too since this would result poor understanding of audiences. To understand the new audiences in Bangladesh we thus need to look into the contextual meaning of new media for Bangladesh. Because it is clearly noticeable that a mixed group of population in Bangladesh are owning personal media through which they are witnessing diversification of global and local media contents laterally with the radical shift in technology and mobile services. Together, these are creating a big move for the audiences of Bangladesh towards a more interactive communication between them and their medium, diverting them from old-fashioned mass communication only.

In this Chapter, I will deliberate different strategies specifically tailored to understand audiences in present Bangladesh society. What are their expectations? How do we measure such expectations? How to explore the modern audiences and their potentials? What business strategies can be used to generate ideas for content from the audience? How can the audiences, thus become a part of content creators? How such trends can create and change new marketplace? A theoretical framework will be shown and discussed to frame these queries.

Finally, strengths and characteristics of modern audiences from Bangladesh will be identified and how they can be used for exploring the potential of electronic media development will be addressed.

———————— • ————————

LEARNING FROM THE CHALLENGES

Research has shown that audiences gave different results on their perception about the media contents[1,2]. Why different viewers tend to give different interpretations of the same content? Several factors like social and economic situation, gender and ethnicity, etc. can be named here as some of the symbolic resources which are associated with these variables.

In today's information age, however, if we analyze audience responses solely based on the media content, only then it will create a catastrophe in a content generation. In today's media environment, people like to engage themselves with the content, regardless of the type of platform or medium they are using.

So what is the right way to look into discovering how audiences are thinking or feeling?

In exploring this we cannot ignore that even though the service for audiences are changing, the audiences remain and will always remain central of this analysis[1,2]. That is to say, regardless of what kind of contents are being produced and what type of medium are being used; it is after all the audiences whom the central focus of analysis remains. Therefore, I believe, in finding the right way of learning the new audiences and their requirements is more a methodological challenge.

The choice of methodologies is not always easy. It is like when we send our kids to a school that we like, we think that it is the best school where my kids are going even though we criticize that the whole country's education system is going nowhere. Likewise, audiences may think a TV channel is really bad but can reflect their favorite program part of that channel to be simply the best. If they do not like anything they will not hesitate to see it disappeared or else the overall blame can be given to the whole channel. So in one methodological aspect audiences can response a program to be their favorite while in another setup of methodology the whole channel can be reflected to be poor by the same audiences. Because of this, I consider we need to go back to the end of this dilemma and navigate back.

If we know that methodology determines the audience awareness, we can say it is a challenge for the media professionals. So for this challenge, what can we learn and then point toward? We simply can generate an improved methodology. Since a proper methodological implication means more reliable feedback from the audiences and this can lead towards an enhanced understanding of them[1].

Therefore, it would be satisfactory to conclude here that audience study methodology design is the tangible challenge from where we can learn and identify new factors that can, in turn, be used to design proper methodology.

Doing so can recognize the contemporary audiences in an ideal manner. In this respect, maintaining a close relationship between researchers and audiences is going to be an important issue for the future. This would help researchers to design their research and study of audience analysis in a style where they would be able to mix different available methods for getting the advantages of the complementary nature of diverse methods. This is specifically important for Bangladesh because using different methods can deliver focused perspective on the reality of different audiences and after collecting different standpoints using different methodologies, it becomes easier for the researchers to be reflexive to conclude how different findings can complement each other since future research on the audience would probably give more importance on consent instead of a specific media side.

So what could be those factors that can make a methodology for audience analysis better than they are at present? I believe this is a contextual question. However, for the context of Bangladesh and present new media revolution era, there could be several alarming issues that experts could prioritize as challenges towards understanding the modern audiences which I discuss below.

Standardization

Two TV channels may have similar or different audiences and using the same methodologies for analyzing them may not be so sensible, therefore. Individual TV channels and their cross platforms should thus focus on designing customized and focused group methodology for audience analysis that can be ideal for analyzing their own requirements.

The measuring audience is multifaceted but this complex process can be made a little easier if we can divide the problems from a relative perspective and then solve them in different slices.

A definite type of channel can have its own customized standardized methodology that can make the audience measurement much easier rather than using a universal measurement methodology. For example, a TV channel focusing only on news broadcast cannot possibly use the same methodology in a successful way that in a music or sports television channel is likewise being used.

Retention

Storing and retention of sensitive information is a key to successful methodology design for audience analysis. Today's computation tools are more powerful than ever before.

Using relevant past data can be a great use to analyze how present contents are behaving on audience insight.

Creating big data for TV channels is the next big thing that is going to happen over time in Bangladesh. Media companies can increase their ability to retail their quality of contents that can be analyzed and represented by advanced statistical operations.

Retention in the media business is thus can be seen as a powerful strategy that can be used in scheming better methodology for improved result.

Real Time Updating

For a successful retention to happen, it is important that media organizations are up-to-date about the market situation, relevant competitors and market trends for constantly evolving in the competition. In Bangladesh, the media market is competitive and thus producing something unique to stand out of the crowd is challenging.

Keeping media professionals and their organizations up-to-date can help them realize enhanced phenomena to add values in audience exploration methodology.

Return On Investment

In spite of everything organizations always aim to return on their investment. The media business is nothing special or different than any other businesses and proving the organizations of TV channels to be effective in the competitive market for gaining moderately fast return on investment is an imperative issue. These issues should be considered and included in methodology design for audiences. It is after all the audiences who contribute in returning the investment for media business owners. TV channels should track other similar competitor media organization's return on investment and find their own unique factors in this respect to adding standards in their methodology design intended for their attribution.

Cost Analysis

In today's information-technology-biased media organizations, the technologies are continuously evolving. Extensive research is needed to get updated and adapted to this ever fast growing technology that is being extensively used in all respects by new media.

In this respect, analyzing the cost of technology is an important issue. Because if technology cost is not analyzed, included and researched the return on investment analysis would be defective and this, in turn, would create problems in the design of a methodology for media organizations.

This is also important for participating in the increased competition in the similar fragmenting market from other media organizations and TV channels. This analysis is now taking a major shift towards social media which cannot be ignored too because a majority number of smart audiences are now internet dependent in Bangladesh.

Ignoring the internet would be like considering it as a black box for media which cannot be compromised anymore in today's media business.

Business Model

Even with proper cost analysis and return on investment strategy, it is impossible to imagine a satisfactory harmony between production and marketing in the media business without determining a proper business model for the organization.

What would be the time span to get a monetary return? What issues are surrounded in need and expectation between clients, agencies and the media organizations? Under the fragment of an effective business model the methodology design for audience, understanding would also be effective, focused and feasible. Otherwise, the whole idea would be only talk and no proper action with any operative result.

Media Research

Media industry faces numerous myriad issues rather than only understanding the modern audiences. These issues could be political or cultural. Then again, issued faced in Bangladesh media industries are not similar to that of in Japan. However, the media industries in Bangladesh at present do not properly address the problems they are facing.

Why is that? Because there is no proper heuristic media research for individual organizations. It is the high time to identify and prioritize the contextual and not- contextual problems in media industries. Doing this research would discover different valuable factors that could be used in methodology design for audience analysis and can turn it to be a feasible iterative design process.

Seeking New Opportunities

One of the problems in Bangladesh media industries is that policymakers here do not want to look beyond the traditional thoughts. People like to follow things that they and their older generations have been following. People are afraid of trying new things and do experiments. This limits the scopes for media development and consequently needs to be fragmented. Finding new opportunities by looking outside the box and limited scope will always pay back with something positive and new ideas could be produced as of this.

Asking queries outside the traditional scope can continually generate fascinating methodological characteristics from which thought-provoking concepts and trends of audiences can be fetched and conveniently utilized.

———— • ————

WHAT AUDIENCES REALLY WANT

Even with the best methodology in hand for analyzing audiences, there is no guarantee that media professionals will be able to understand its audiences, since as I have mentioned in the previous section, this process is highly contextual and dependent on many diverse factors.

It cannot be neglected that the success of our content marketing is reflected when our audience responds to it. But there are certain characteristics of modern audiences that should be taken as the basis of the analysis, especially while dealing with a social setup like Bangladesh.

Since by doing this, further analysis can become more flexible with the higher reliable output of result. As in today's market, it is not enough just to say audiences expect entertainment or updated news information from around the world. Their expectation is more complex than this. Moreover arguing to provide what the audience need, can be more contradictory than providing what they want since it is difficult for media professionals to determine what is best for their audience by themselves.

How many times you tend to tell yourself and your surroundings that there is nothing on the TV? Then again, how many times you were so focused on a program that you did not realize you had a phone call or the doorbell rang or someone came into the room? Audience behavior changes so rapidly.

Like I pointed out earlier, even with the proper methodology in hand how credible the audience research can be? In a populated country with several demographic variations in Bangladesh, how many families can a researcher reach for their study of the audience? Can it be the right sample size for a generic conclusion? Is market research enough anymore in this respect?

Even with the emerging research strategies like neuroscience, biometrics, ethnography and behavioral economics, the power of internet dominates and overrules the era of traditional market research. Besides this, we must now consider what kind of devices audiences are using. What could be the context of use for audiences when they are using a phone comparing to a tablet device, their desktop and on a TV. Audience focus, the center of thought and nature of relaxation now varies on the type of devices they are using which also creates a key impression on their expectation.

As technology changes, its acceptance should thus be viewed through the lens of audiences. What do present audiences expect together with such familiarities? What would be the expectation of the prospective audiences? Since investor's expectation also changes with technology familiarities and their expectation analysis can help us filtering the unnecessary requirement to be implemented for the development of the audiences.

So at present, it is more than asking questions and trying to measure their answers only for audience expectation analysis. To materialize this, some fundamental properties of audience expectations for modern audiences are therefore needed to be documented and therefore are described below.

Trust in Media

Understanding the lack of trust in the media is important for media professionals and the researchers, because only then can they contribute in creating better media. Audiences want to trust the media and that is the fundamental entity for them to act and interact positively with the media. Do audiences want to know and trust that something has already happened? Present trends in Bangladesh show such examples that media professionals here want to study what has happened.

After a certain event has occurred or executed we like to create reports on them. It is, however, equally important to be proactive for the media professionals gain increased trust from the audiences. Academic researchers can play a crucial role in this respect by trying to bridge the gap between stakeholders (audiences) and media professionals (journalists).

Identities

While audiences expect to receive information to meet their need they also feel the need of realizing what kind of diffusion would be created for individuals and society by the innovative production of the contents.

Audiences want to receive an objective understanding of the both sides of the arrangement of media content creation and its impression on them. Media professionals in Bangladesh must realize that identity has become more fluid and transformable over time in this age of globalization.

One and a half decade before when the first private TV channel was introduced in Bangladesh, audiences were viewed as a resistant towards social changes and remained analyzed in traditional ways. Now that trend is broken and media today barely focuses on tradition and in its place, it is looking onward. The generational gap is another issue for shaping the value demands of modern audiences. Online identity has created a lot of different options for individuals to explore themselves.

For these reasons audience identities at present is seen as emerging properties of diverse characters. In this respect, one important thing not to forget is that representation is one part of identity that can reveal the identity, but it may not help audience construct their own identity.

Modern audiences expect to discover their personal and cultural identities of the individual and collective identity perspectives. For modern audiences, identification is a variable that can construct and evolve over time, which the mainstream media professionals should consider with great importance in media development.

Participation

While TV content is now being distributed on different platforms the interactivity level of the audience and their networking has augmented than ever before. The electronic media broadcast system at present in Bangladesh is undergoing a big shift and this is going to alter its structure and role. With this shift, the character of the audience is also changing within the context of the audience participation, which now defines a variety of connotations. Audiences sitting before TV set are barely considered as a consumer or spectator anymore. The traditional meaning of TV has turned to be more "social TV".

Audiences have the abilities to use multiple, sophisticated devices for their participation, which are getting cheaper for mass populations to adapt. This expectation of participation for the audiences is higher than ever before in today's world since this is empowered by technology, which enables different types of audiences to contribute in contributing.

People expect to use social media and broadcaster's website to increasingly and interactively engage themselves with live shows. This is because audiences like face to face interaction and they feel increased trust and cooperation through such dealings and relations. Media professionals should act on this for getting used to on the prompt modification in our present digital environment. This will revise the viewing pattern of the audiences and in turn, their potentials in an iterative manner.

Control

Modern audiences anticipate more control and by their power of identity they want to understand themselves to be the character of a specific scenario for altering and interacting with a precise storyline. Since today's media are connected to the web, the outdated concept of the owner or creator of content is taking a swing. Audiences in this respect, for example, would like to have more mobile apps for complementing their traditional TV viewing experience.

Content generators and media professionals do not at present have clear ideas about audience need or what really do they want, which is why the audience should be given a chance to talk with the content generator. By that way, audience will feel they are in control and will appreciate how the media organizations can be out there to aid their commitments.

Successful Presenter

Audiences are exposed to presentations and they like to receive information to meet their needs. In today's media era presenter is not playing the role like presenters in the earlier time period. Audiences expect that presenter gets to the point soon and they want to get a clear impression about how the content delivered by the presenter will help them and why those contents are vital to them.

What I believe is going to happen in media in the near future is that by the power of social networking and other improved means of the technology for communication, audiences would like to play a role of structured communicators with the presenter. In this way, audiences will want the presenter to tailor the information that they would be seeking to serve any specific necessity of the audiences by understanding their different attitude, beliefs and opinions.

———— • ————

OPEN AUDIENCE INNOVATION

In the previous section I raised a question about determining the need of audiences parallel to what they want. As we have discussed, realizing what they want involves methodological complexities while determining their need by the media organizations are confusing too.

I believe in today's world, it is not enough for the people with authority (editors, reporters) to have this power solely instead audiences should be given a chance to be integrated in the decision making procedure. By that I do not mean the audience will provide what they want or what they need only, instead I mean they should be involved in the development of content generation.

This is because, we can raise more complex scenarios instead of asking what the audience want or need by asking ourselves what information are out there in the community[8] that is hidden or unknown but can be facilitated by the professionals, to find out and then implement? As a remedy on answering to this open question I will introduce the concept of open audience innovation in this section.

In this respect, I have used the concept of open innovation[3] where internal and external knowledge is brought inside an organization to improve its own internal innovation aiming for market expansion through external innovation exploitation. At times, it is difficult for organizations to rely on their internal research which is when a research driven generation of intellectual properties are needed.

By doing this kind of open innovation the cost of research and development for the organizations can be reduced while productivity improvement together with the ability of using synergy and accurate market research potential are some of the other benefits that are offered[3, 4]. These advantages are traditionally triggered by the involvement of stakeholders in the early phase of a development process.

On the basis of the previous complex discussions on audience requirements and need along with the methodological contextual complexity, one ideal solution could be to let the audience be a part of the content creation process on the basis of the open innovation concept. That is, media professional can use their audiences to generate ideas for content which then can serve the purpose of their need and expectation. As a similar example, Starbucks can be mentioned here when they have used their customers to generate ideas about what different kinds of coffee drinks could be out there that customers would like to see from the Starbucks. They have generated the ideas from the customers and later introduced some new drinks in their store.

Although the process of involvement and getting an output is not an easy one, it is promising for the society of Bangladesh, where the large population is out there to support and get involved in such concept and can result a pragmatic solution to the problem of audience requirements.

The principle idea here is that we want to see a reduction of the gap between audience desires and requirements. If we are able to do it through creating improved content, then audience satisfaction rate would increase resulting improved productivity. Thus, a way to look into the open innovation concept[3] through the lens of audience requirement and need analysis for improved content generation could be interesting.

For electronic media market in Bangladesh this concept can be a key to success since the organizations there are always striving to come up with something new and unique.

Because of the rapid social media movement along with improved and cost effective communication ability turns the audiences of Bangladesh to be a potential focus that could be feasibly used for content generation using this concept.

But to realize how we could get the most out of this practice, we first need to learn some basic principles of open audience-innovation with respect to the contemporary society and new media which I introduce below.

Gap Reduction

With open audience-innovation as a target for a media organization, a goal should be specifically fixed. It is not very simple that organizations can think they will use audiences to generate ideas for a content generation rather they need to justify and fix what purpose that content would serve.

Which is why understanding the real need and requirement of the audience is desirable because without that it would be difficult to frame the problem for the audience and they would end up contributing their knowledge in a style that may not be appropriate for the organization.

In the same way, if too much desire is reflected in the project plan from the organization, then audiences would lose confidence in themselves to contribute towards a productive result.

A reduction of the gap between the desire and requirement should thus be analyzed at the beginning of the organization aiming to initiate open audience innovation. Understanding actual and perceived needs of the audience are a key issue in this respect.

Simplicity

Why would an audience like to participate in a content generation if the process is complex- this is the type of question the professionals should ask from the audience point of view before designing open audience innovation projects. For the ease of making the process easy, organizations should make sure that audiences can find relevant information easily.

Simplicity in information finding can make a positive reflection from the audiences on immediate and long-term decision making in content generation. If organizations provide crucial information properly to their audiences, it can help in reducing the gap between desire and requirement from content that will result in an optimistic attitude for the audiences towards contributing in content generation.

This is the key property of open audience-innovation if we are to see some radical changes that external innovation can bring for the media organizations.

Alternative Evaluation

However, presenting proper information to audiences is important, but not always enough since audiences would like to evaluate similar information or analyze similar content from their past experiences.

Providing such powerful alternative ability of evaluation already to the audiences by the organizations would open up whole new opportunities for idea generation through the audiences. The simple static information would barely tickle the audience's brain while comparison ability with several similar contents would open improved communication channel between different stakeholders and ultimately leaving a positive impact on gap reduction between desires and requirements.

Transparency

Transparency is important for triggering audience psychology in a positive way. If the information provided by the organization to the audience is limited they may perceive the information differently. If they discuss this with other stakeholders it may create a negative impact for the organization and is will impact poorly on the future productivity.

On the other hand, audiences may alter their own thinking on the content they just have contributed in creating, by the consequence of post-contribution behavior. Providing transparent information from the beginning would thus reduce this risk and thus organizations would not risk themselves to get irrelevant information or start the innovation process from the start.

Balancing Parameters

We already discussed how complex the audience need or requirement assessment can be and that, it involves several different variables and conditions. While all these variables cannot be realized and used by the organization for their audiences during the innovation process, it is important that they try to maintain a balanced flow between different variables while creating information to be used by the audience to trigger their perception towards content generation.

It could be maintaining a group of variables or reducing the gap between different variables since the success of content creation through open audience innovation would depend on the total associated variables effect.

Audiences then should be able to assess themselves based on these variables and be able to approach from one factor to another for understanding their identity for a successful contribution in the innovation process initiated by the organization.

Efficient Solution

Even with the best innovation process, it cannot guarantee that audiences would understand the problem in an error-free manner. How the designed innovation process would affect the overall business model of the organization is not always predictable.

The organizations should, therefore, be prepared to give efficient solutions to different problems that may arise during the course of the innovation process that is both internal and external to the organization. Audiences would then show increased efficiency through their innovative capabilities.

Organizations should also have internal expert panels to deal with problems after the innovation process is completed and if needed for the efficiency of the outcome, this expert team can contact stakeholders to update any information that they might be confused about.

This would also give audiences' confidence towards trusting the organization and gaining credibility on the contents they have innovated.

Simplicity for Convenience

Simple information presentation to the audience adds value to the information for the flexible and efficient use of them by the audience. This can surge the convenience of the content to be generated by audiences. However, providing ease to the audience is again contextual and can vary from different content to content.

But once it is successfully provided it can increase productivity and improve the collaboration between different stakeholders. Different targeted contextual goals set by the organizations in the early phase of the innovation can, therefore, be achieved by this principle.

———————— • ————————

NEW AUDIENCE, NEW MARKET

So far I have discussed the paradigm of new audiences with their expectations and how audience themselves can be a part of a content generation to take care the problems of uncertainty about the need and thereby dealing with different methodological complexities.

However, it is clearly understandable that with new audiences comes the new market. Even with the best methodology in hand and open audience-innovation in practice, the end product can be less usable if media professionals do not understand the news segment of the market. Some discussions about new market within the context of new audience need and their activities are therefore narrated here.

From previous discussions, it is clear that media organizations face clear challenges that are related to the audience measurement of different TV channels for causing effectiveness in their content generation. Media organizations also feel a challenge from other similar competitors.

This worries their own business model and then it turns out to be the biggest challenge of all. Audiences also often find a gap between media organization's promise and their marketing agents. Many organizations also find they have limited scopes to expand towards new opportunities. I believe these problems can be summarized through the lens of one big problem. If the organizations can keep themselves updated with the present market trend other issues could also be taken care then.

— • —

It is, however, not so easy to flow with the fast evolving industry that is producing novel competitive complex market. I in this respect would like to stress the strong point of the notion of niche market[5, 6]. On the concept of a niche market, a specific thing is focused on the perception of a subset of the traditional market. In media industry, this concept is highly practiced already. In Bangladesh, we are watching application of such concept- dedicated TV channels for news is an example of a niche market. Another example is ESPN or Star Sports TV channels which exclusively focus on audiences that are enthusiastic about sports.

Now based on the different characteristics of new audiences different complexities associated with them as discussed earlier, it is also important to stress how the marketing segment and an idea can be taken a different shift parallel to the fast evolving technology and rationalized audiences.

Important here to realize is that with rapid technological advancement, audiences have become niche too. When there was one private TV channel in Bangladesh the mass marketing was practical. Now niche marketing has taken a gradual shift.

I believe in the survival of existing and future electronic media in Bangladesh, the primary focus should be given on niche marketing in content generation and broadcasting. Otherwise, audience frustration would continue and they would carry on departing to watch the local TV channels. For example, news TV channels are already popular in Bangladesh and they have been able to divert the audience's attention and focus from other overseas news channels to the local news channels.

Similarly, TV channels highlighting only sports related programs has gained popularity because of a huge population group in Bangladesh that enjoys watching this on a regular basis.

However, the key challenge in the respect of niche marketing[5] and dealing with modern, niche audience that still remains is the issues of content generation. While a dedicated TV channel creation concentrating on certain interest is always an option, it is a big contest for the present media world to create niche contents to be a fit for purpose in regular TV channels that are covering news, sports and entertainment programs.

So the question remains on, how can we successfully define the target market to be the appropriate one for our niche audience? There is no golden rule for answering this question. Nonetheless, advancing the analysis of market from traditional to contemporary one is the first step.

Organizations need to realize what the real problems are and not just the perceived problems. Media professionals need to dig deep to realize which groups of people will be most seriously and adversely affected because of this problem. Once they have a clear idea, these groups of people could be categorized and grouped through their common properties. Then the appropriate market concept could be thought based on different properties, namely audience categories, geographical locations and flexibilities associated with different market sectors.

Organizations should then look internally to explore what expertise they own? Are they good in dealing with a specific group of people or are they expert in a specific location? Also, organizations should look into other options and opportunities externally to analyze their credibility in dealing with the complications.

Nevertheless, it requires a lot of analysis regarding how, why and where audiences interact with contents. Complex analysis can identify and segment the appropriate market along with its significant audience.

Some of these complex analyses can namely involve requirement determination for content fulfillments, obtaining external survey data and do in-depth analysis for drawing complex conclusions, collecting internal data for diversifying perspective on advanced marketing efforts for maximizing return on investment.

Marketing online is nothing new in today's information age and the concept of affiliate markets can also be a powerful way of implementing the niche market concept online. Online journalism practices can also be very powerful and effective to act as the market driven journalism[7]. All these factors and phenomena can be extremely useful in analyzing and understanding the appropriate market for the new audiences.

We cannot ignore that audience is the central element of media study and marketing strategy cannot be one static issue for audiences[1, 2]. Since audience types change over time, so should the marketing strategies.

To successfully realize the proper marketing strategy in this dynamic, changing audience focused media world, organizations should also focus on issues like audience fragmentation, their specialization, and diversity.

Identifying the proper market for the proper audience would then be successfully reachable.

———————— ♦ ————————

PROFESSIONAL PRACTICE

I n this section, I show a theoretical framework to fragment the audience related issues that I have introduced and discussed in Chapter 1. With all these theoretical concepts in hand, it is important to understand how to implement the concepts in real world problems dealing with the audiences. A framework can, therefore, be convenient in this respect.

Figure 1 below tells the story of how different characteristics of modern audiences can be taken into account towards a successful content generation for increased productivity.

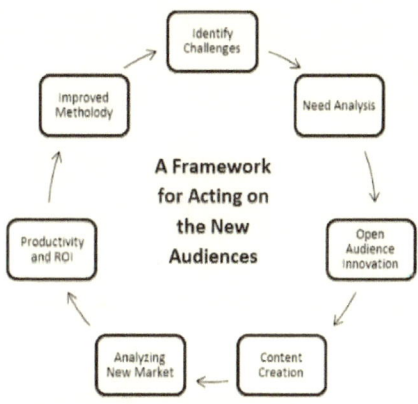

Figure 1. A Framework for Acting on New Audiences

On the top of the framework, I have placed different challenges from which we can understand the audience. We can proceed to realize audience needs from here. There are fundamental needs that are stationary for modern audiences and together with the lessons we learn from different challenges and audience need and requirement analysis can give us a holistic insight into the audience and their expectations on different media contents.

Next, I have presented that based on the previous knowledge gained about the audiences they can be involved in the content generation process using the conception of open innovation which is titled as open audience-innovation.

Successful application of this phenomenon would lead towards effective content creation which would open up whole new opportunities to create a new market for the new audiences. Effectively identifying the proper market would increase productivity for the media organizations representing towards enhanced return on investment.

Finally, all these gained knowledge and experiences could be used to generate an improved methodology for audience analysis. This in return would help us identify different novel challenges from where we can learn new possessions about the audiences. Consequently, this process can then iterate over time.

Even though the nature of this framework is highly theoretical, it has its own potential. As discussed earlier, an important challenge lies in creating and using the appropriate methodology, the focus of this framework is ultimately pointing us towards contributing to the methodology improvement.

However, it is difficult to take this framework and try to empirically study on an existing media organization setup. But if an organization would like to analyze new audiences and their novel trends and want to use this knowledge to practice open audience-innovation for improved market creation, intended for higher productivity, then this framework can be an essential tool for providing the right path of such research.

Also, it was mentioned earlier that challenges and need are complex and contextual phenomena. This framework, therefore, can be practiced in the scenario of contemporary society's media organizations since audiences are different in different media setup. So this framework is not solely meant to be used in Bangladesh media setup only rather it can be tested and used in organizations that are fragmenting their content generation and media studies, based on the frames illustrated in Figure 1.

———————— • ————————

EXPLORING THE POTENTIALS

In the concluding part of Chapter 1, I want to stress that the success of my discussion on modern audiences will be effective only when we can explore the scopes of different potentials in real world practical problems in media development. But then again, it is highly contextual too. Still, within the context of the contemporary society of Bangladesh, the issues addressed in this Chapter replicates enormous potentials.

Our audiences now are smart, alarmed and connected to the information superhighway. At present people in Bangladesh are more concerned about whereabouts than ever before. Because of political instability, people find it tempting to be included in the political discussion. The Internet and social media use have taken a huge shift in recent time. Mobile internet usage has dramatically reduced its cost while the cost of mobile devices is dropping too.

From rural to city life, students from primary education level are learning and using a computer which was not the case even ten years back only. Concerned citizens are not always relying on watching TV instead they are on the go and can procure and share information from their mobile devices.

Social media in recent time has proven to be a huge, powerful tool in providing different news and discussions among the concerned citizen. With all these ongoing in Bangladesh, it can be positively extrapolated that the factors discussed in this Chapter can be of high potential for media development in Bangladesh. No doubt there are dissimilar hitches associated with effective execution of this process, but carrying them forward is beyond the scope of this book.

Audience measurement is a complex issue and it can for sure vary from one country to another country, one culture to another culture. Political and legal issues of the different country along with their established policies can impact on the environment of the business models of their media organizations. But then again two markets are not same.

Asking simple questions like what is a story about and who does the story affect and how, who has the right information and can put it into the context, can make a big difference in realizing what audiences need[7]. If content generators can answer these themselves then audiences will be able to detect them too. These actually indicate directly towards the audience without focusing any groups, insiders or any direct participants.

Potential audience analysis can be subsidized using the power of computation. Regarding this, analyzing audience tweet habit, data mining of the social media content for content analysis of potential audiences, analysis of followers can give us insights about a group of audiences, their preferences, and lifestyles. In this respect, the concept of computational journalism will be discussed later in Chapter 5 of this book.

———— • ————

One of the critical barriers to entering into the broadcasting market is understanding audience behavior. There are already dominating broadcasters out there in the present Bangladesh electronic media market and those who want to enter the market as newbies have a very short and critical time to create a base with the audiences by offering something attractive to convince the viewers. The new concepts and trends that were discussed in this Chapter regarding new audiences and their potentials can be a powerful point of departure to break the different barriers of traditional audience research in Bangladesh for taking us few steps ahead in this ever fast, rapidly changing and technology biased world towards the achievement of improved content production.

Chapter

PERVASIVE PERSUASION

"Persuasion is clearly a sort of demonstration, since we are most fully persuaded when we consider a thing to have been demonstrated."

-Aristotle-

Imagine you are in a cloth store to try some clothes and did not want to buy them for whatever reason it may be. Now what if the salesmen become aggressive and start to hit you for not buying clothes from their store? How would that function?

It would not function at all. Instead of doing such, shops gives us attractive offers and discounts that motivates us to buy things. Use of physical force for achievement is replaced by persuasion in the rational world.

Every individual in society persuades and influences each other to move forward in reaching their individual needs. Presidential candidates promise different things to persuade people and get their votes while organization manager encourages its staffs by indicating higher productivity-persuasion is everywhere.

There are tons of influences that are functioning in our society to make us believe and act on doing different things that those influencing agents want us to believe and act on. This persuasion phenomena are often non-detectable by the people in general and even with some awareness people tend to not care much about it as they believe they have more freedom to take decision instead of being persuaded by others.

It is, however the influencing agent that frames the persuasion for managing the situation of the individual's response on which the success of persuasion primarily depend on.

Persuasion has been related to the media industry for a long time, although the nature of persuasion took a different shift as the time passed. At present it is not anymore, primarily focused on creating advertises to attract consumers. The pervasive nature of persuasion is one of the key concepts to use for audience psychology understanding, motivating them and involving them in creating better contents for electronic media.

In Chapter 1 I have discussed about the characteristics and potentials of new audiences where I have argued that it is more a methodological issue. We saw how audience behavior is changing with the technology shift.

Now, to support in generating improved methodology and different methodological factors, we need to understand how modern audiences should be treated from the cognitive psychology point of view because psychology is significantly used to understand the different implication of technology. In this Chapter, I will, therefore, discuss different scopes, possibilities and aspects of psychology that can be used to bond between audience expectation and content generation.

What factors to look and how to analyze them? How can

experts trust audience perception to be intuitive? Are there any specific patterns that can be followed? What cognitive model can be a handy tool for the experts dealing with these issues? What needs to be considered to explore the electronic market and internet users? These subjects will be briefly explained and deliberated here.

The concept of pervasive computing and its related research aims of generating smart products for modest communication. I assume that the successful implication of the pervasive nature of persuasion that can be used in electronic media would therefore aim for improved communication between different stakeholders and media professionals for generating smarter contents in smarter marketing environment.

The structure of this Chapter follows like this. At first, I have discussed electronic media psychology and some of its characteristics from a pervasive point of view. Then persuasive design for the media content generation is introduced where I have established persuasive design principles. Next, I have developed a cognitive model for persuasive media content generation and elaborated it.

The psychology of media and my derived model and principles were then used as a point of departure to initiate a discussion on bonding between audience and content from a cognitive point of view. After this, the notion of intuitive perception of content generation and its importance is stressed and discussed. Finally, the concept and potential of cognitive marketing exploration for the success of a persuasive media content generation is discussed. In different sections of the Chapter, Bangladesh electronic media is used to exemplify some topics of interest.

———————— • ◆ • ————————

ELECTRONIC MEDIA PSYCHOLOGY

How we human behaves with the relationship with our media is the general question that the researchers in media psychology ask[1]. We have seen an explosion of new media in over last two decades, which has transformed our society dramatically and the challenge now is to understand our experiences in this world surrounded by an explosion of media.

Different theories of psychology like perception and cognition are the foundation on which media psychology is established upon. The target is to generate a working model after critical analysis of user perception on media experiences[1].

However, with the rapid shift of technology mediated audience perception, I believe the traditional way electronic media psychology has been looking into different analysis needs a change. It is not enough to establish a hypothesis, conduct experiments and quantify collected data to understand the impact of media on individual and society. I in this section will discuss electronic media psychology from a pervasive point of view.

The aim is that, if we could make a move forward of the traditional media psychology concepts in a pervasive way, then it would be easier to make use of these characteristics in persuasive design.

Then a working cognitive model would also be possible to generate flexible using which the audience and media profession relationships for improved content generation and market analysis could be effectively initiated.

Cognition

In a simple way, cognition means thinking, but there are obviously different forms of thoughts. The pervasive nature of cognition can explore and identify different patterns of thoughts that can be powerful to be used in media. Considering a holistic viewpoint on learning, creativity, understanding how memory works in media perception scenarios, how different sensory perception can make sense of content creation, how to take advantage of embodied cognition, dealing with proper reasoning and decision making and handling biases properly could be integrated in the thought of dealing with media content generation and its relation to the consumers.

Human Behavior

It is after all our behavior that is the core of all understanding of content and reflecting on them. Humans have interest on reward and they have a certain level or reactivity on the reward. Also, humans are impulsive and they are goal driven. It is important to take these matters into consideration for improving the content design. Are our audiences goal driven?

Are they motivated by their behavioral approach? How impulsive and sensitive they tend to act on certain content? How about if individuals are not receptive to rewards, how to deal with them for turning them to be a successful audience of your content? Or how to design content, thinking that special subject groups in mind? Once we look from this perspective, it would be easier to identify audience characteristics based on their mood, desire and other simulations for generating content in a persuasive manner.

Emotions

The role of emotions in effecting media progression for the different beneficial outcome is no new field of research. However, with the changing audience and technology, emotion and its effect should be regarded from a different point of view. What is the role of positive emotions comparing to mixed emotions in persuading audiences? How can we use this knowledge to generate improved content? What could be the role of emotion and how to deal with it in generating content that makes audiences make a decision?

These issues are not easy to answer and should be analyzed from a micro level. It is, however, possible for media professionals ask themselves these questions during dealing with a specific problem of program creation for example.

This property of media psychology is extremely important for an emerging society like in Bangladesh, where at present it is important to analyze why we interact with media the way we are doing now?

It is, however, my expectation that to understand these complex but extremely important issues, we look beyond the data collection and dealing with mathematics only and use personal experiences too in generating content by dealing with pervasive properties of emotion.

Technological Development

Integration of the pervasive nature of cognition, human behavior and emotions should not only be used for content creation but can be a great tool for requirement analysis towards the development of new technologies.

This is a process that human-computer interaction (HCI) research field has been focusing on but new media and its development are now highly viewed through the lens of HCI. Due to the competitive academic environment blending different disciplines for generating something new is a common practice in today's research world. The traditional gap between researchers and practitioners should be eliminated when it comes to new media development. For this, new technology development can also take a big shift through the power of pervasive cognitive psychology characteristics that are useful in bridging different research disciplines.

For Bangladesh society, this phenomenon is extremely crucial for the integration of different types of people in the society with the technological development so that they can adapt it as it happens.

Dynamic System

Considering the use of media psychology for improving stakeholder's relation and thereby improve content generation for productivity cannot anymore be seen as a single event rather it is a part of a complex dynamic system. If an analyst considers this process on the basis of a slow or reflective system, then the output would generate a more objective element of a specific situation.

On the other hand, a reflexive and conceptual system will identify important vital elements in a situation. Important therefore is to think from the perspective of mind towards the development of media and not the other way around. Due to the power of the internet and social computing, it is impossible to consider a media system of today not to be a dynamic one. One way of doing this would be to look beyond the era of mass media to practice media psychology.

User Responses

With the advancement of technology, content production is changing which also is changing the way contents are perceived. Now user response is what technology and content perception are dependent upon. This is extremely important because the survival of media is dependent on how good we are capable of controlling and holding the users since they are the one uses technology and view our generated contents.

I believe the aim of future media professionals should be to reduce the gap between user response and content perception along with the technological development. If users are driven by their individual motivation and judgment this gap would be different. Professionals can imply different types of bias and persuade through their content design for controlling user response.

Neuropsychology

Understanding the structure and function of the human brain in relation to the process of media development is a complex process. But we have seen similar research in the area of accounting and marketing, for example. Non-clinical settings of Neuropsychological studies for understanding how the human brain behaves in terms of content perception and audience reflection can open a whole new paradigm in media research.

Different cutting edge medical tools like MRI, CT scan, EEG and MEG with elegant software for conducting studies in Neuropsychology[6] can be used in academic research of media using the experimental psychological methods. I believe, in the very near future this practice will be popular and one of the common practice in understanding the advanced meaning of persuasion, addiction, fear, attention, relation and attachment style together with other different social interaction within the context of media usage and stimulus.

Content Production and Perception

Although media psychology does not focus exclusively only into the content generation and it looks into the holistic characteristics of the whole system the content production is always going to be important of that big system. Since the whole system and the parts of the system are dynamic in nature, there are several emerging properties and synergies occurring and the process of content development thus becomes a part of a continuous loop.

The success of improving the content and its perception from the audience perspective can be benefited by looking outside the box of cognition, behavior analysis and dealing with different actions between the media environment. Since these are all coexisting together, it is difficult to isolate them and then include in a design.

The goal should thus be to make sure that different properties that are beneficial for a content generation should be pervasively presented in our analysis.

Communication Improvement

Communication is a broad term in the media business. Audience communicates with live programs, a presenter communicates with the participants and with audiences-sometimes even in nonverbal ways like facial expressions and body motions. Stakeholders communicate with content generators in different ways.

The challenge here is to make communication improvement process a pervasive one that would be built in the media psychology concept. Practicing debate may be good, but introducing a dialogue is probably going to end up in a better communication with a productive output towards a solution. It is very important that a story based, goal oriented focus is practiced for the successfulness of communication improvement. Validating other people's experience by allowing them to feel safe and establishing a dialogue frame can be extremely powerful in communication improvement. These properties should be remembered and practiced pervasively in media psychology studies.

Tools Development

With all different characteristics, I have discussed so far here in media psychology section apparently the aim of creating different tools for media research that can, in the long run, help promoting different media technologies in a positive way. Tools should be developed, improved and customized to improve communication between individuals, societies, and nations[1]. The improved tool can help us implying methodology in an advanced way and the understanding of audience for content improvement process can positively be triggered by this. Within the context of Bangladesh, this is also very promising. The competition and limited scope in different TV channels are a major issue in Bangladesh media at present. Similar content creation and repetition along with copying other's idea is notably occurring there.

Designing customized tools for individual TV channels for

a specific group of TV program generation can give the media researchers new insights in improved and unique content generation.

————— ◆ —————

PERSUASIVE DESIGN

The core concept of persuasive design is everything about crafting diverse experiences that can influence people's behavior. Persuasion is defined by Fogg[2, 3, 4] as "an attempt to change attitudes or behavior or both (without using coercion or deception)". We see the effect of persuasive design in many sectors of our everyday life. Mobile apps are designed to persuade us to walk to bike instead of driving a car there by doing well to the environment and being health conscious.

Different campaigns trigger our thoughts to act for sustainability and do well for our environment and economy[5]. In media development and research study persuasion is greatly used. As discussed earlier, it is all about handling the audiences and generates contents according to their need and creates a successful market based on the technologies.

Nevertheless, research showed that as technology develops rapidly, a significant underlying problem of persuasive design remains to be its inability of understanding proper design strategies for a system aiming for a focused target behavior. I believe the issues with persuasion and media is not an exception to this either. Persuasive design in the media needs to look out of the traditional concept of creating content to lock the audiences only and by thinking like this a lot of new complexities could be identified in media persuasive design.

However, in this Chapter I am stressing the importance of the pervasive nature of persuasion for which in the discussion of previous section I have identified several factors for understanding and exploring the pervasive nature of media psychology. Now I would like to discuss persuasive design within the context of media study- involving users and their content generation for higher productivity from a ubiquitous point of view.

For this, I would like to emphasize on three key factors of persuasion that were used to establish the Fogg Behavior Model (FBM) [1]-motivation, ability and triggers. In this model Fogg argued that motivation and ability work together in a behavior and if the individual's ability is increased it would impact on their behavior performance instead of working only on the motivation.

It is however important that without an appropriate trigger a specific behavior would not take its place even with the right motivation and ability[1, 5].

I argue that these factors should pervasively act on media content, design where persuasion is aimed to be practiced. Based on this assumption I have derived some persuasive design principles for media content generation as discussed below.

It is assumed that if the following design principles are practiced in designing content, the persuasion will be better and more successful in dealing with making a difference between success and failure.

These design principles thus would act on balancing motivation and ability of individuals while initiating an appropriate trigger to them too.

Equitable Use of Resources

Balancing resources or if needed, minimizing them is one of the best strategies in design.

The success of shaping and balancing performance of a designed system would depend on the resource uses. Sometimes a group of people can be a resource too, and it is important to balance the performance of individuals in a group.

Media organization cannot expect to generate a cutting edge persuasive content while it negotiates with the resources that are important to create such content. Similarly, the excess use of resources where it is unnecessary would not result in a great content to persuade either.

In involving user groups in a content generation it is important for individuals to see that the changes of attitude that they have adopted are also followed by others in the group or else they can be less motivated and not appreciate their involvement in the process.

Increased User Inclusion

Media content generation is always for the mass population. Although content can be for a focused group of users too still usually it is designed with a bigger group of population in mind. Therefore including most possible audiences in the process of generating content is highly desirable.

Persuasion should be occurring at the individual level, it is true, but it is apparently meant for changing the collective attitudes of a group. At present content generation only focuses on people who are physically and cognitively healthy. How about a bigger population with different types of disabilities? Different types of disabilities are increasing over time in the society while people are getting older and their longevity is increasing too.

There has already been being a big demographic gap between younger and older people in the society. Although younger people are using technology more at present, this trend will be broken. A large population group, who will be older, but healthier and older or younger people with disabilities, will then be left over with no appropriate contents created for their purpose.

Design for all paradigms should thus be considered while thinking about media content creation.

Mutual Capabilities of Users

A persuasive content in the media cannot be complete if user inputs don't consider throughout the design process. After all, it is for the audience (users) for whom the content is meant for.

One of the primary mistakes today's media professions does while they generate contents is that they think they are the audience of that content. So they end up liking what they produce while the mass population as audience avoids seeing that program on TV.

While looking through the eyes of an audience is a good approach to design it is also important to include user-centered design concept in content generation. The audience should be given if possible, opportunities to easily customize and understand the design simply to give their input and feedback.

This would increase the possibility of the end design to be successfully persuasive enough for the target audiences.

Respect Privacy

Maintaining user privacy is nothing new, but for media, content generation understanding user and their plays a different role. At the age of the information superhighway the definition and role of privacy have taken a different shift and dealing with this issue ethically is more complex than it sounds like. In an open audience-innovation process, for example, user behavior detail should be respected and the user should be given an assurance that their data will be protected and that there is no chance of any adverse effect with their sensitive information.

This would work as a motivational trigger for the users to include them in the process of content development more enthusiastically. Users would then be gaining the ability to perform their natural behavior which is important for the media professionals to identify, observe and understand.

Maintain Transparency

Organizations should be transparent about the content that audiences are working on, the content that is being produced, about its purposes and effects on audiences. Being transparent to its audiences is one of the key persuasive characteristics that media organizations can do.

This, in turn, can shape audience behavior in the future for a better content generation. Also, audience can gain trust in a media organization because of their transparency. As an example, presenters who actually represent a media organization can also be transparent in their presentation, discussion and involvement with audiences, which acts as a powerful trigger for user motivation and giving them confidence in their abilities.

Media researchers and content designers should keep this important issue in mind since this design principle can generate advanced contextual strategies to understand and justify audience target behavior that was aimed at the content generated by the media organization.

———————— • ————————

A COGNITIVE MODEL

The discussions from media psychology and persuasive design section can be integrated under the hood of a theoretical framework which results in a cognitive model for persuasive content generation and will be illustrated and described in this section.

I have used the characteristics of media psychology together with the properties of my five design principles of persuasive design for media content generation together with the three factors from the Fogg behavior model[1] to structure the proposed cognitive model. Figure 2 illustrates the model.

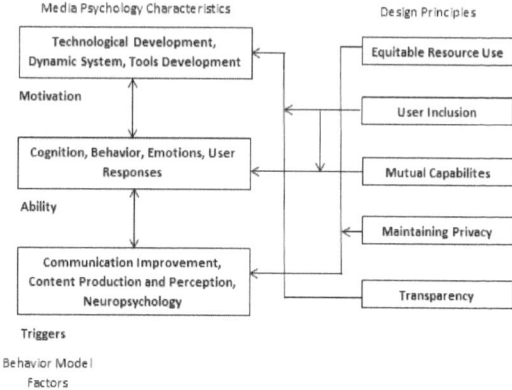

Figure 2. A Cognitive Model for Persuasive Content Generation

A path diagram is used to show the relationship between different entities in the proposed cognitive model in figure 2. Different media psychology properties were grouped under the three categories of factors from the Fogg Behavior Model[1]. Then the identified five design principles were shown on the right side of the model in relation to these three factors. It is assumed that if this cognitive model is followed or taken under consideration during content generation the nature of the content will be logically persuading for higher productivity.

One important aspect to remember here is that it is not a process but a model. It can be used to approximate the human cognitive process specifically designed for media content generation. It can help us predict different things associated with content generation and development. It is a way to simulate how media professionals can solve their content generation problem and what would be the ideal mental processes that could be involved in ending up with a successful persuasive system. It is also possible to improve existing content by analyzing them using this model. However, a design life cycle can also be derived if needed for this proposed cognitive model.

Different technological development and tools developed for the progression of the dynamic system of media research and development can be a powerful motivation for the media professionals and audiences. Increased user inclusion and being transparent with the users would trigger these factors.

On the other hand, an individual ability like cognition, behavior, emotions and users' response to a certain matter is categorized under the ability factor from the behavior model.

The inclusion of different groups of user and allowing them to use their mutual capabilities would trigger this factor. Finally, improved communication, production of content and its perception together with Neuropsychology are categorized under the trigger variable. Equitable use of different resources and privacy maintenance of the user would stimulate towards initiating a trigger for persuasion to happen successfully.

———— ♦ ————

AUDIENCE AND CONTENT BONDING

Understanding the connection between the audience and the content is the primary reason why we need to look the problem through the eyes of psychology. More emotional audience connection leads towards driving more engagement from them.

Moreover, the content in the electronic media is becoming more personal. It is thus important to understand what media professional's role could be to drive this matter. Talking with the audience always is a good idea since their feedback regarding an organization's service has been valuable.

Creating unique insights should also come from the organization and this will help in direct communication with the stakeholders. Extensive use of humor, empathy and compassion could be valuable too, since the power of emotion is extreme in bonding creation.

Audiences expect the media organization to be an expert in content creation, but sometimes it is not enough only to show that an organization is an expert. Instead, it is important to show evidence to strengthen the points reflected through the content. Maintaining credibility for being objective and professional is the key to bond with audiences.

Also important to remember is that the relationship between journalists and audiences, are also changing and so is the nature of the content, as journalists are content generators too. This relationship is more interactive than ever before that aims to meet different demands of the audiences. Technology, social media along with other uses of digital media now makes it possible for journalists know what are the desire, expectation and interest of audiences. We see practical examples of this in the electronic media in Bangladesh.

But then again, journalism is at the same time losing its "journalism values" and thereby its economic values too, since people do not trust in journalism the way they used to do before. If we can restore credibility and trustworthiness together with more accountability and authenticity by practicing transparent journalism, then these issues could be dealt by the media organization and their editorial departments. This problem is also reflected in today's media industries in Bangladesh. Because of the business nature of media viewers are considered to be the customers while understanding them is sometimes compared with marketing. But in reality, the citizens of a country are not really customers. The main idea behind audience satisfaction with the content lies in the fact of trust- audience needs to feel that the content that they perceive is true and honest.

It is all about creating a relationship with the audiences through the content, whether it is news or any entertainment program. These contents should hold certain qualities like values, judgment, authority, intellect, courage, commitment to the community and authority[8].

These characteristics can psychologically trigger audience perception and content generators should thus consider these. This is especially critical for Bangladesh because too often the goal here is a commercial success instead of practicing true journalism. Media organizations can make a difference in focusing these parameters during their content generation by gaining audience trust by creating more credible content for them. These parameters could also be statistically verified to assess a specific content and analyze its bonding with a group of audience in the society too.

It can thus be concluded here that, to gain back the trust through transparency, traditional approach may not be enough in this age of new media and using the new digital approach would thus be more appropriate. The use of the cognitive model and analyzing the issues through the eyes of media psychology as discussed in this Chapter could play a crucial role in achieving this.

———————— ♦ ————————

INTUITIVE PERCEPTION

Our ability to analyze and grasp something instantly by perception is called intuitive perception. Through this, we realize the reality around us.

I think media research has neglected the important issue of considering intuition in dealing with the decision-making process. It is, of course, a challenge to create content that is for real valuable to others. Nonetheless, it is important to realize what adds value to the content that makes it valuable.

While perception is about understanding something, intuition reflects the ability to know something instinctively. Intuition works for the present moment during the merging of concern mind with our physical body.

Media content generation can be highly benefited if intuition in perception can be considered in the design. If audiences can use their power of intuition to perceive the contents, then organizations can get the most out of it for their commercial benefits.

However, this is a very delicate process which requires a lot of psychological studies to come up with new design principles models and frameworks. But contextual content generation for a society likes Bangladesh, where the education rate is very low and there are high demographic differences for people living in rural and city areas, this phenomenon of intuitive perception could be a trump card in successful persuasive content creation.

A program that focuses on the rural population by covering their specific interests (agriculture or rural music, for example) can use those audience group's intuitions to create captivating contents to get the total attention from them. An academic or complex political debate in TV talk shows, on the other hand, can gain knowledge of the backgrounds and abilities of the focused, educated audience groups to manipulate the show contents for its success. The presenter of these two example scenarios can also play diverse effective persuasive characters by taking the contextual intuitive perception abilities of the target audiences into consideration.

Even so, one of the prominent problems, when audiences are communicating with media content, is that they suffer from different cognitive errors.

During perception of the content, audiences can fail to practice their rational and reasonable thought and behavior. Audiences are often used by the strategy of the social proof in talk shows or in advertising for example. These can take a different shift if we can use the concept of including intuitive perception in designing. Dealing with confirmation, authoritative and even survivorship biases in content creation could also be improved by applying intuitive perception.

However, what actually is important for the audience and how can we create a marketplace for that will be discussed in the next section.

———— • ————

COGNITIVE MARKET EXPLORATION

Reading an extravagant and catchy title like cognitive marketing has always been fascinating, but realizing the importance of the concept is more significant.

Before grasping what cognitive marketing is and what its potential can be in a media context, it is important to ask ourselves, what do we really do with traditional marketing? We sell different things. But how about selling stuff and trying to improve people's lives? How about selling things that are really important to the consumers? These are the basis of the cognitive marketing concept.

It is no doubt that computing power has increased along with big data and individuals with more connected devices and sensors on the internet. These issues are simply the triggers towards a new marketing thought and cognitive marketing is the new and the next big thing to happen[7].

It is the concept of marketing where understanding the emotions running through the mind of consumers are the basis of creating more meaningful advertise or campaign. Traditionally, digital marketing has been successful in capturing our eyes with beautiful and appealing design, but we barely have other cognitive abilities to analyze a situation.

Our ability to feel, smell or taste is not possible in a digital campaign. Cognition is the additive that is missing from today's marketing which will be able to diversify and open new scopes of promoting new media and its success.

One of the interesting characteristics of cognitive marketing is its ability to provide the consumers, things that are needed by them. That is to say, allow us to acquire items when it has a purpose. This is highly promising in media research and content generation.

Media organizations can use computational power to analyze audiences to figure out what program or advertisers are desirable to them. This is where the transformation of media psychology study takes the shape in a practical form of application.

Can audiences be given the option to choose what they want to see and what they do not want to see by allowing them to customize their profile on a TV channel website? I believe the organization for sure would see higher productivity by doing so. Why audiences in Bangladesh are at present so against watching local TV channels and transferring their interest towards overseas TV channels? How can we get them and their interest back to our local TV channels?

What happened actually was that the local TV channel organizations have pushed different content solutions without thinking too much of selling tangible items to the audiences and did not care about how the Bangladesh society as a whole would receive the holistic message of doing such which has invited the unavoidable dark image to their organization. Cognitive marketing can be a resource for rescuing our audiences from such a deadlock situation in Bangladesh.

In the concluding paragraph of Chapter 2, let us fantasize something. Imagine that your favorite coffee brand lets you see they're commercial while providing you an opportunity to smell their coffee at the same time through your smartphone sensor. Or when you see a new perfume advertise on the TV you are given an option to smell that scent too. How do you believe these two content provision preferences would trigger your mind from a consumer's point of view?

Acting directly on your cognition through successful cognitive marketing as exemplified here may still be a science fiction, even though it may not be so far away from the reality, but the proper framing of content for cognitive marketing can for sure control our perceptive sensors autonomously.

CHAPTER

3

CONTENT EVOLUTION

" Nobody will have control of the media in the future,
because user-generated content is going to become the
major content. "

-Jimmy Lai-

Understanding audience needs, expectation and their behavior with the advantages of different cognitive psychological factors can be strength in media research and development only when we can transfer this new knowledge into content development and improvement.

After realizing the modern audience and their psychology the next practical approach would be to integrate these knowledge for value-added cutting edge content generation.

This Chapter will highlight these aspects. Media organizations need to work on their content development, according to the market need. Also, organizations need to realize the types of appeals needed to be created through their content for public to consume it[2].

What is important to realize is that content development is not an arbitrary episode instead it is a continuous process. If we want to see improved content, then it is important that the content generation process should also be improved. For electronic media content development, this is a sensitive issue as content can facilitate social changes. This kind of change is highly likely to happen in a country like Bangladesh that has a diverse group of population in terms of their age, education background, and socioeconomic situation.

These things are also affected as technology changes rapidly. On the other hand, the power of ICT has different disadvantages with respect to different factors like cost, credibility, familiarity and it is important for electronic mass media to arrive in optimal communication for giving rural development efforts[1].

In this Chapter I, therefore, will highlight issues related to content creation and development within the context of new audience and new technology for the contemporary society, especially focusing on the electronic media of Bangladesh.

I will take an attempt to analyze the process of audience research to content creation up to the marketing and try to shed some lights on understanding significant issues like drawbacks with present contents in electronic media in Bangladesh, their reasons for being a problem, their impacts on the future media business success, importance for Bangladesh media professionals to stress the importance of content generation, scopes for shaping the basis of quality content creation and different associated risks in this process.

How can we take full advantage of audiences and their psychological perception to create cutting edge contents for Bangladesh electronic media?

How to draw finest conclusions in understanding audiences? How to choose a critique group for evaluating contents that are designed to fit for purpose? How to compete with the others in terms of business and commercial success within the context of content creation and management?

These issues will be discussed in this Chapter. A theoretical design space framework for a future content generation in electronic media will be proposed and discussed to explain the methods and processes associated with effective content evolution.

But before we dig into the analysis of content and its development let us take a look at the importance of realizing what do we really perceive when we use the notion "understanding". Because it is the fundamental concept on which the core idea of audience perception and the success of the content marketing and thereby regenerating improved content depends upon.

———— • ————

WHAT IS UNDERSTANDING

When we observe or read something do we need to "really understand" it or is it enough to be satisfied by internalizing the knowledge from the content? Or is it important just to grasp the essence of the story? What difference does it make for an audience who really understands or just grasps the essence? How often content designers think this way before they plan and analyze the outcome of their content? I barely believe it happens in reality.

It is, however, extremely important to think this critically. Nobel Prize winner Daniel Kahneman in his book Thinking, Fast and Slow[3] referred the notion of narrative fallacy from the book The Black Swan[4], written by Nassim Taleb to explain the continuous attempt of humans that make sense of the world.

According to Taleb, we tend to fool ourselves by creating false or weak assumptions about the past and then believing them to be true. Kahneman also discussed the role of halo effect where we tend to judge on one attribute that is specifically significant by ignoring other qualities[3]. Negative halo effect also exists where if we do not like one attribute we tend to dislike the whole qualities. Imagine when you change your TV channel and see your favorite anchor is on the screen. Even though you do not like the content of the talk show you still become the audience of that show because of the audience. Similarly, just because you do not like an anchor can make you switch the channel even though the content of a show is your favorite.

Audiences are a learner of the content, media organizations deliver to them. The elements between the learner and content should be minimal so that the learning process can be easier. But in practice this gap is huge and there are so many factors to consider between learning and content.

The primary reason is that we do not really agree on what understanding actually mean to us. We assume we understand the past and we can know the future too, where in reality we understand past less than we think, we do[3].

In a content generation, it is thus imperative to realize what kind of understanding the media organization is going to create. Content developers should be careful about the ambiguous use of the phrase "understanding". Our mind creates the best possible understanding using the available information around us and if that understanding is good we tend to believe it for which knowing little information can help joining the puzzle bits of creating a coherent story[3].

Realizing what understanding really is can be the most complex task for media organizations that are developing content, but this process can be made smoother by using different assessment techniques. In fact, the nature of understanding is slippery that is always changing, dynamic in nature and the audience has their own imaginations on this notion which is why it is important to consider with great importance by the media organizations.

CONTENT ISSUES

The content creation as I stated earlier is a process rather than one event only. The process involves multiple steps and can iterate over time. However, for analyzing and identifying the problems associated with the content I believe it is not fair to blame the industry only instead the problem is to deal with the people involved in decision making and content writing.

Lack of vision and planning is the main problems that are reflected in today's media content which in turn fails to create a successful market and audience attention and finally productivity.

One interesting aspect of the Bangladesh electronic media industry is that the audience there tends to divert their interest to watch programs on other TV channels instead of the local ones.

The Younger generation in Bangladesh often becomes obsessed with the character of a TV program from the neighboring country. Even there are records and evidence of committing suicide for not getting fashion products that are used by their favorite character. What kind of content other TV channels from neighboring country with similar cultural values are producing to divert audiences from Bangladesh is a burning question and is not the scope of this Chapter, but it is important to identify the problems with the present electronic media contents in Bangladesh.

I discuss some of the aspects of such problems in this section. It is important to realize that instead of blaming the content that is already generated, we need to go back to the root of the problem where content generator and management should be given the focus. So while discussing problems with content I also discuss below the issues related to the authorities who are responsible for creating content.

Uncertainty of Quality

Organizations tend to use external experts to create content for them. Then it becomes the question of quality. This is highly evident in the Bangladesh media industry. For commercial success, only organizations can sacrifice the quality of the content and can accept the contents from external source just because it saves their budget. Clear cut specification about what an organization is expecting from the content is, therefore, important in this case.

Source Awareness

Similarly, when external people create content it is not always obvious which sources they have used for their production.

How can media organization, be sure that the person they have hired actually did the work? There is a risk that the hired person wanted to deliver something from another source and then justify his or her payment for the work he is hired for. Allowing credible people to submit content can resolve this problem.

Time Restriction

Involving audiences, customers, and fans can be a great way of generating unique content, but then, on the other hand, it costs additional time and effort from the organization end. So it is important to combine quality, source awareness together with time planning ahead of time. Like any other important project, content generation should also consider the time management factors with great care. Because negotiating with the time can mean compromising with quality and then the problem of source credibility can also arise.

Active Participation

User generated content (for example, the open audience-innovation process discussed in Chapter 1) can take the organization's content quality into a next new level for which intensive planning is required. A good strategy and management of time and resource are important to make the process successful. It is easier to have a great idea to make audiences involved in the innovation process, but to get them actively participated and engaged in the actual process is another thing.

Sensationalism

Often media organizations focus on creating stories or program content that is sensational. This often can involve violence and scandals. The content generators focus on these so that their story gets sold while in reality, it can create several adverse impacts on the audience. It is not wise to create a content to sell only instead of valuing its importance and requirement to the audience. Over time the audience would thus lose confidence and reliability of such content and can divert themselves to other sources.

Poor Coverage

Focusing on sensation often leaves the media to forget things that are happening in our daily life which we really are interested to know more about. It is true that people in Bangladesh see a lot of talk shows discussing politics as it is one of the major parts of the life for the citizens of Bangladesh, there could be other contextual and focused interesting and important coverage issues that are neglected at present.

For example, it is interesting to see how much coverage of news and TV programs are made for promoting environmental issues and concerns? How about health and education issues? Creating a program on TV where a doctor answers the questions of the audience in a live telephone conversation is not at all covering health in a holistically way.

Similarly broadcasting issues about education in talk show is not also a representation of education in coverage. In reality, what happens is that content creators neglect what they have agreed upon to create.

They know that they as an audience would like to see things like this on electronic media, but when they are in charge they tend to go with the flow. This impacts on the quality of the resulted content, therefore.

Lack of Experience

It is difficult to find a content generator who is expert and has deep knowledge in the field of a specific interest that media organization is planning for. This in turn impacts on the uncertainty of the quality of the content. One way to deal with this issue is to look internally at first place, within the organization.

A multifaceted content generating task can be broken into smaller parts where different experts within an organization can contribute in creating quality smaller pieces of a content that can result in a perfect end product.

If externals are hired for content generation, then they can get insight with the people working in the organization so that the topic and its depth can be analyzed and assessed by the people working inside the organization for improved outcome.

Audience Understanding

Like software designers often ignore the user of the software, content designers ignore audiences. Knowing your audience is the one unique trump card that can help content generators creates perfect and successful content for their organization.

It is important to remember that content generators are also the people responsible for adding value in marketing the content that they produce. If they simply think themselves to be a writer then they sacrifice quality of the content.

The researching audience is thus imperative to realize what their requirement is and to deliver content that can meet their needs.

Because of the lack of this, media organizations in Bangladesh create content with the flow without understanding the need of their audience and thereby lose the audience. Thus providing the content writers with as much information about the industry and audiences from an organization can possibly pay off in the long run.

Lack of Motivation

Lack of motivation creates poor output. For many professionals that are involved in generating content, it is a routine process that goes with the motion and quite boring tasks, which ends up with a boring result, therefore. An organization can easily blame the CEO stating that the person has no motivation and is less productive. But then again it can be looked from another perspective that the CEO feels that way because the other persons constituting the organization are also boring and has no motivation either. Blaming on management cannot solve the issues of motivation.

Analyzing deep during content creation can thus result in interesting outcomes. Humans are always interested in new things and digging deep through research can produce interesting results in the form of in-depth content with stimulating styles. At present media industry in Bangladesh, most of the authorities are generating content for the commercial success and for the sake of running the process of the content generation which is why the local audiences are so frustrated about it. It is important to change the strategy of content development and is thus important to allow the content writers plenty of time to research the industry and audience.

Uncorrected Mistakes

Studies have shown media organizations are quite poor in informing audiences about errors in their content. Good content opens up the opportunity for successful content marketing and it is an essential part of succeeding. The errors in the newsroom along with other factual errors need to be taken care carefully.

Often organizations lack in staffs taking care of error

handling only even though it is a crucial part of content creation. Media organizations, thus need to give correction more prominent display and should maintain internal guidelines for making corrections for the credibility of their created content.

———— • ————

CREATING QUALITY CONTENTS

Issues discussed in the previous section can be seen in a way that since they are the drawbacks of content at present media industries and if we can eliminate these, the content would be improved and be of better quality.

While this is true, it is also important to understand the elements of such process while we eliminate these addressed issues.

In this section, I will introduce the characteristics and elements of contents that can be called high quality. Important to evoke is that if we understand the audience and their use of technology, then the quality gets refined often within the context of media organization, culture, and society. What was a quality content a year back may not be quality content today? The concept of quality content is nothing simple for the success of marketing only, but it is something organizations and policymakers strive for all their professional life.

While some strive for creating relevant content only, it is contextual too, since relevant content can also be low in quality. Partial high-quality content can be impacted by the poorly generated content from the same source and can overall impact the content to be poor. Some of the aspects of creating quality contents are discussed below.

Blending Media

Content has multiple representations. It is thus wise during content creation to mix different media. It is not about the articles only, but multimedia, photos, videos and slide shows are also an amazing way to engage audiences. Besides, individuals learn differently. Blending different media uses are thus important to help illustrate an organization what their points are.

It is, however, important to note that random blending of media is not suggested and the use of multiple media is feasible only when it adds additional values to the content. After all, it should be aesthetically pleasing to the audience. Social media share at this information age is a must and can add tremendous value to the content marketing.

Also, rapid mobile technology expansion demands the ability to deliver content ready for numerous platforms like TV, smart phone, and the web browser. By doing this, content can be used to offer more to the audience since the good content would increase demand for them. Ability to give feedback and share is important in today's social media powered cyber world and these give the audience more engaging triggers to get the most out of the content.

Adding Values

The target should be to give something to the audience so that they can educate themselves while at the same time they get entertainment out of the content. This can be done by delivering a focused value in content generation.

What is out there for the audience and what benefits they can get and how can be more captivate for audiences to get locked on.

The addition of more content to create a holistic representation of the focused content can help too. It is important to ask if an organization can produce content to solve any problem or answer any question or just to provide unique expert insight. Or is it that the target has only been to make people laugh or entertain them?

Either way value creation should be there and aimed from the planning phase of the content development. Useful and informative information is the key in this regard. At the same time, it should be more valuable and resourceful than other similar content generated by competing organizations.

Original research behind content creation can add credibility which can earn audience trust and reputation.

Originality

Ideas should be original and this is the fundamental trigger for creating quality content. Creating original content can give organizations the return for years and help motivate in a similar development.

A tendency in Bangladesh electronic media at present is to go for a quick fix. Content writers and the policymakers look for a cheap solution, outsourcing by sacrificing quality, collect articles from web and permission to use them which hampers the overall quality of the end creation.

The neighboring country of Bangladesh in their electronic media business produces rapid original things that create a psychological impression in the audience- they find that their requirement gap is already filled up with the content from the same source even before their current expectation is finished.

Decision makers and media professionals in Bangladesh should take these things under serious concern so that competitive original content can trigger local audience's interest.

Using trusted, authoritative source for backing up content can allow the media organizations leading towards accuracy.

Actionable Content

What is important is that the audience gets a realization of what they can do and how they can transfer the knowledge they learn after watching content.

For instance, a TV program focusing on health or the environment should not only give the audience some valuable information, but it also should open the consciousness of them so that they can learn and use the knowledge that they have just acquired.

If they cannot use the facts to improve their health issues or cannot learn some dormant subjects about the environment, then the whole idea of such content would be void. Focusing on the goal and intent of audience is the primary thing content creators should be looking into.

The quality content is the one that actually gives the audience a sense of how to apply the information. The content should not dictate the audience and tell them what they need to do; instead, it needs to motivate them to use the material by respecting their wishes. This implies for generating internet content like blogs too.

Engaging and Thought Provoking

Engaging audiences are the best thing content can do. In a TV talk show not only the topic of the show can engage the audience. For some individuals, the topic can be very interesting while for others it can be boring.

How to captivate the audience those who think it is boring? The presenter can play a crucial role in this situation. The presenter can leave audiences with questions, have a promising and important introduction to initiate curiosity on the topic and can start telling stories instead of reading written scripts only.

These are crucial factors to turn even a boring content to be a thought provoking one that can successfully engage the audience.

Presenters should also be ready to provide the answer to the queries they ask. People participate in the discussion and think it is interesting simply when they get answers to their questions. Presenters should be smart enough to scan audience perception to rapidly pick up the interesting facts for quickly acting on reciprocal engagement during the discussion.

———— ♦ ————

CONTENT VALUATION

With new audience come new psychological perceptions that help us create new types of content. Now this new type of content needs evaluation too because it will then help us understand the audience and their role in building the methodology furthermore as I have discussed in Chapter 1.

Our ability to encounter the media from plenty of a number

of sources raises the question of which one to trust actually? Besides for the sake of marketing success content requires reviewing.

Different stakeholder demands are rapidly changing while parallel to this new media development process is also going on. It is imperative to demonstrate the effectiveness of the content of the management of media organizations for them to take a further important decision.

The management level decision can be supported by good measurement which is when the valuation part of content comes into discussion. Several research methods, guidelines, principles, and rules along with frameworks are already out there for media content evaluation. What I in this section will, therefore, be focusing on specifically is how to evaluate media content for the Bangladesh electronic media sectors at a present time.

However, this discussion can also be generalized with other country's perspective given that the contextual similarities of the situation are identified.

I believe with the speedy, ever fast popularity and development of the internet and mobile culture in Bangladesh the future of content will be satisfactorily be focusing on social media contents.

This is because media organizations in Bangladesh even were forced to distribute their content in the social platform. So the trending nature of content in Bangladesh is the distributed content. I, therefore, suggest giving a major emphasis understanding the importance and evaluation of distributed content. In this respect creating customized tools for the content publishers for evaluating their content and requirement on where to publish is important.

One of the primary characteristics of evaluation is to set up the objective properly because the whole process and its result would depend on the objective. Identifying the objective to be distributed content evaluation can be a key for Bangladesh media organizations. This is because the management should take distributed content and social platform as a strategic issue and not just a quick trick to grab temporary attention.

Because mobile technology and social platform are going to control the information distribution over time media organizations should adapt this change by altering their business model.

The mobile app report from the comSCORE 2015 identified that smartphones and tablets now account for 62 percent of all digital media time spent. Mobile contents are faster and interfaces are attaining better as the graphics processor power is increasing. Mobile platforms are obviously larger than traditional news agencies where news and entertainment like we see on TV is a small thing compared to the whole bunch of other things mobile technology can offer and does.

While the present TV industry in Bangladesh is struggling in capturing and holding their audience for not to slip away for viewing other country's content, a fundamental shift has already slowed taken its place in a social world. Content evolution in social world can thus create next big marketing success and the proper content generation in social world can also get the audiences back to their local TV channels.

Like I have discussed earlier, Bangladesh is a populated country where a huge gap in educated and non-educated people is prominently visible. Due to poverty and lack of proper rural development yet, internet and computers are not reached in many places.

For a huge population, TV is therefore still the main source of entertainment when unfortunately that audience group is also losing interest in the local media. For these population groups, content evaluation should be rapid, intensive and more critical now.

In this respect defining the target audience is important by asking where is the audience located, why they like or dislike content, when it is relevant and important to them, in what context and who the major target audience are. It is after this when the key issues that can affect the organization and the field of business can be identified. In this respect, it is important to share the findings from such research with different managements of the organization to get important insights about the result and data.

And finally, then the result can use to improve the content for the audiences for which it is meant to be.

In summary, it is important to note that when the audience is so diversified and rapid technological and social movement is going on in a populated country, it is difficult to generalize audiences for content assessment. If we try to apply traditional media content assessment methods, then chances are that there will be biases in our result.

The situation in Bangladesh TV audiences is two folded. A group can be categorized to be advanced- using mobile technology, always connected to the internet that likes to see on demand content and is an advanced audience in terms of choosing their content and device. Another group can be categorized as the traditional audience who are fond of contemporary TV viewing but are distracted towards satellite culture and diverting themselves to other country's TV content.

Thus, it is possible to categorize audiences in Bangladesh in different genres and not just these two categories as I have mentioned here. These two categories can be further broken down and so on. Analysis and evaluation of content for Bangladesh audience should focus on this genre level analysis. It would then be possible to look into critical issues for content like violence, cultural values, minority representation, stereotyping etc. By doing this, professionals can overcome the problem dealing with explicit biases regarding content perception from the audience perspective.

FUTURE BUSINESS SCOPES

While mobile technology is replacing personal computers and social computing is beating traditional searching, new trends and business scopes in electronic media like TV is taking its shift too.

Future business scopes are created as the content is improved and evolved with the smart, advanced new audiences. The question is thus if we are or we are not ready for taking a shift to such future commercial possibilities. Swift innovations due to the fast technological transference and never ending expectation from the audience can be a threat for organizations, but it can also be an opportunity for those who are ready for this change.

I believe it is a high time for Bangladesh media organizations to get ready for such challenges and consider them as their opportunity. Bangladesh has all the required resources like other developed countries; it has got talented professionals too. What is required is thinking outside the box of traditional scope and grasp the opportunities. In electronic media content generation, I believe the media organization should extensively focus on social media.

Augmented reality, live video, the ability to text and participate, social advertising, social video as a mean of communication should be more open and instantaneous. It is important to remember media will create a role and it will always matter as long as human exist, but the question is if media organizations will be able to survive or not. It is probable that if organizations are not coping up with the trend someone else will come and fulfill the requirements of the audience that others were incapable of providing.

Though focusing on mobile and social computing would open a lot of new business scopes it is important to remember audiences would like to devote for experiences. A regular 2€ coffee on the street costs 15€ on top of the Eiffel tower and visitors still pay for it.

Do they only pay for a coffee or they pay for purchasing an experience to drink coffee on top of the Eiffel Tower while watching the beautiful Paris, even though the price of a small cup is insanely high?

Audiences will be ready to spend on gaining experience and media organizations should be ready for these. Humans have an innate content craving and they want to feed that in new ways and not the traditional forms only.

Forthcoming business scopes are often initiated by the new technology development. From the perspective of content in the electronic media organizations can get an impressive payoff if they are ready for exploring the scopes only.

However, it is important to remember that combination of different electronic media can have improved advantages over isolated electronic media usage.

Therefore, my discussion above should not be interpreted only as a call for reaching social media dramatically for the media organizations in Bangladesh but to engage themselves with audiences by the power of social computing and the application of different technologies with the help of a new generation of tools, that can facilitate them to be prepared for competing with other global media organizations.

———————— ◆ ————————

A NEW ERA OF COMPETITION

Now with the new scopes of business raises new competition. Maintaining a competitive edge is then important and staying ahead of the rivals is the survival factor in the media business. It is thus important to realize strategies to survive in the competitive media market environment. It is getting more and more difficult to survive in the heavy competition in the media business and constantly improving strategy can help the organization to separate themselves than others.

Notable issues related to competition that is visible in the Bangladesh media world is that organizations are too obsessed about their competitors which apparently makes them unproductive.

However, knowing the competition is important because it is possible to learn from other organization's mistakes revealing new opportunities in the marketplace.

This is because other's mistakes can be modeled as a solution from an organization's perspective. Competition can trigger earning more revenue too.

The subsequent points are my recommendation for surviving in the new era of competition created by the new audiences and quality content.

Knowing the Competition

It is important to analyze similar organizations and their competence to see what they are offering to the market that is different. This analysis can help an organization identify the things they need to focus on developing for altering or re-identifying unique selling point. If the talk show of a TV channel is popular then a less popular channel should analyze that talk show to understand what kind of content they are discussing, what are the strengths and competence of the presenter and guests so that they can improve their own content.

On the other hand, creating something unique that an organization's competitors do not do are another way of empowering the competition. A small confectionery store in your local neighborhood is always busier than a super store. Because the small store understood the essentials that consumers like to buy more frequently. The Same analogy can be applied to the successful media content generation for organizations The Clear and obvious contrast from other similar organizations on the basis of competence is important for the quality content creation and the productivity.

Marketing Setup

Without proper marketing setup to let the world know what an organization can offer is not going to allow the organization to survive in the competition. Why should people watch the TV program of a channel? Why is it unique? What is in it for the audience? Organizations need to work on letting the audience know about these issues.

There are strategies of marketing that does not have to be

expensive either. Marketing in social world can be one of the key strategies regarding this issue. What an organization does best should be presented to its audience. Important is to identify something unique that differentiate the company from its competition and use it as a key marketing strategy. Also important is not to forget to offer similar products that an organization's expertise can capable of providing. That is to say, diversification through content creation is a trigger to attract audiences.

It is like restaurants offering free internet access. It does not matter for the quality of the food or for the free internet- people may talk about their likeliness of that restaurant because of diversified services they offer. As an example, Bangladeshi audiences interested in education may get benefited from an academic TV program, but they will also love to see programs that inform them about the process and regulations on studying overseas.

New Market Exploration

At the same time, it is important to capture multiple markets to expand the sell and earn audience attraction. By focusing on multiple markets the risk associated with the business can be divided. If an organization creates TV programs that can be seen on TV only then the risk is to lose audiences who are more used to using mobile devices to watch content.

If an organization can spread its content generation plan towards the mobile platform, then it would be able to catch those audiences and thereby can gain that was lost from the TV audiences.

The converging overseas market is another trick. More and more people are moving from Bangladesh and living in foreign countries for work or family reason. It is not wise to exclude those powerful population groups who are more interested in watching home country's TV channels.

It is thus useless to spend time with people who would never be interested in a specific content as well as to put more emphasis on a target group that is concerned about their favorite content.

Involving into the community and being active is another way or exploring a new market. Media organizations should never forget that in this dynamic, rapidly changing competitive business world visibility is one thing they should not negotiate themselves with. Also, community involvement can define the scopes of being active in the local, national and international community too.

Clever uses of Social Media

The opportunities in the social world are enormous. Organizations are always trying to be better than others in the social world because of the competition, opportunity, and openness are huge there. I believe the small use of social media can pay off organizations. Monitoring of keywords, dealing with alerts, and using RSS feed can be some strategies.

Social media can be used to find out information about the other competition and the key people in another organization. Shared fan interest analysis from Facebook or analysis of Twitter audiences can be a great way to measure and analyze competitor's content sharing rate and their responsiveness against market leaders that can help organizations to attract the smart online customers.

Customized tools can be used by organizations in fulfilling their specific needs and queries. Social media is the type of source where content can be presented and delivered in a way that may not be possible for others to do by building their own platform. Researching competitors on social media should also be considered to be a regular practice for media organizations.

Future Vision

Planning for growth is always going to bring success to an organization. The media business is extremely dynamic and being satisfied with the happy to stay skill will push an organization out of the competition.

It is important to keep up with different development in the specific sector of the media business, whether it is advertising or content improvement. Following consumers trend and invest in new technology to plan the long-term vision, will pay off and organizations can stand out in the crowd with unique experiences created for the audiences.

A DESIGN SPACE

The fundamental problem addressed in Chapter 3 and the remedies discussed so far are represented in the form of a theoretical design space framework for content creation in Figure 3 which is adapted from[7].

Such a design space can be useful for quality assurance, to provide operational flexibility to the process of content creation and then maintaining the standard of the content after the process is finished. The parameters that are used in the design space framework of Figure 3 are logically related to representing their relationships in the content generation process.

While the content creators and media professionals involved in the development process can set the standard of describing the proposed design space framework, the focus in Figure 3 should be given to the representation of important variables and their relation only.

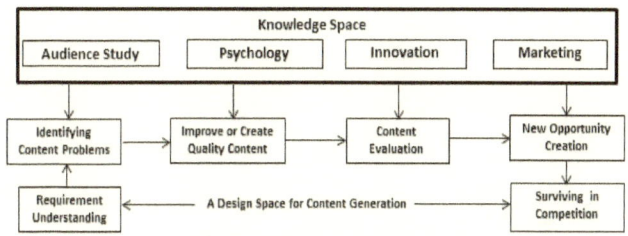

Figure 3. A Design Space Framework for Content Creation

The proposed design space framework can be interpreted starting from the process of building a knowledge space as a result of combinations from audience study results, their relationship with media content and psychology behind it, analysis of the market for focused or a group of audience and then any innovation that is triggered due to all these factors.

Knowledge of this space can then be used to start the process where requirement understanding is the first stage. The successfulness of requirement understanding can make the process of understanding the flaws in existing content smoother.

Together these two can contribute in improving existing or creating new content.

After this comes the evaluation process of the content which triggers new business scopes and opportunities that can lead towards competing with the other potential media organizations in the market.

A need for the survival in the high competition can then again initiate the process of understanding the requirement through which the whole design space can repeat its process again. The figure shows six processes in the form of block diagrams which were individually discussed earlier in this Chapter.

———— • ————

METHODS AND PROCESSES

With a design space framework in hand it could be said that content creation process should be easier or flawless, but in reality, it can be much more difficult than this. With complex and quality content creation for the smart audiences advances the need for improved methods or process of content creation. It is thus important to stress few words about this issue here.

The organization management has specific roles in different stages of the production of content. These stages typically are the development, preproduction, production, postproduction, and pre-distribution.

These stages involve multiple activities- from planning, budgeting, user research, contract writing to approval process and marketing efforts. While these are the parts of a traditional production process and many kinds of literature have discussed these methods, I would like to deliberate other techniques of content generation process that can be ideal for new audiences to produce competitive content optimally and feasible.

The concept of co-creation and crowdsourcing is the number one issues I would like to put my emphasis on. Teaming up with other complement company to create content can be highly beneficial as by this organization can find out what other audiences are thinking about their content. Besides, many collaboration tools can be used today for using many loyal and inspired customers to involve in the crowdsourcing process to same time and still create quality content.

Secondly, the importance of the process towards converting it into content is another vital aspect. If there are a different specific process involved in the development work it could be possible to write down some of those processes in the form of content which will help the members of the development team to work more efficiently. Usual routine processes should not be conducted as a part of a bigger development process instead they can be integrated as a mean of instructional content to save time.

Thirdly, planning the time for content development is one important issue that can define the content development process and method. Planning ahead and maintaining a marketing calendar together can pay off in the process of development.

Planning ahead can help media organizations let their audience know what they can expect and what is going to be released in the near future. Planning a detailed outline of the type of content to be created in the form of a list is important too. The development tool and other stakeholders involved in the process can use the same tools for smooth collaboration and get update about time constraints.

Fourthly, the ability to use pre-designed content to transform it into some new content can be a powerful method of content creation too. It is not unlikely that many organizations have a lot of content created already but are not complete. They can be worked out to spin them off into new content. An existing promotional video can be used to expand another project to add more values for the audiences.

As a final point, content development process should be isolated from the approval process because then the development team can focus on development and not waste any time for unnecessary communication with management. And vice versa the approval of content process should be a simple task so that it does not make the development process over complicated.

This way development team can move quickly to another content creation project with happy audiences and other stakeholders involved.

In respect to creating quality content, authorities should not forget to focus on curating their content too. Content can be good or hold certain qualities to make it better, but that does not necessarily mean it is well organized, properly filtered and designed to always make sense of the information to its audiences. Proper content curation can help manage cognitive loads and that way it can make sense and create social intelligence. Methods of the good curation of content, studies, and looks into different sources for remixing and transforming the best out of them to the audiences.

Organizations thus need to focus on identifying novel techniques that they can use to help their professionals stay focused during content generation. Professionals in the media should blend the concept of content curation in the form of a process while creating contents.

They need to establish a habit for evolving themselves into this process of adopting a new behavior to make "paying more attention" their regular habit. Different tools can also be developed to customize their need for helping them perform better in content curation.

I believe the issues of process and methods of content generation as I have discussed above can be of great advantages for the media industries in Bangladesh.

Rapid content development can allow organizations to realize their capability or limitations for surviving in today's competitive market. The traditional production process is usually followed in Bangladesh but it is interesting to realize that the involved activities in such processes can be blended with the processes I have discussed above in this section. This can be highly beneficial for the productivity, efficiency, and credibility of the media organizations in Bangladesh. However, there are issues with risks that are associated with content which will be discussed in the last section of Chapter 3.

--- • ---

ASSOCIATED RISKS

With all good things about understanding the flaws of existing electronic media content and improving them for better assessment to realize our audiences better using improved methodology the issues about risk still remains there on who is using the content how and what messages they are perceiving from the content along with whether it is appropriate for them or not.

If media content triggers antisocial cognition and behavior of its audience, then it is an alarming issue for the content generators and the media organizations. Understanding different associated risks as the content and the audience gets smarter is therefore needed.

How children and youth are accessing media today in Bangladesh is not the way they were doing fifteen years back. Their frequency of using electronic media has increased which is why it is important to investigate what effect electronic media content creates for them.

There are different social issues involved also. For example, the upper-class society -parents in Bangladesh sometimes have the wrong perception that their children would be smarter than others if they can use the internet.

By allowing their children to do this often parents do not observe what their children are watching and learning. One solution to such problem can be controlling the access to content where it would be possible to break down access and use trends by gender, age, and socioeconomic and racial differences[5].

Because for children, their emotional development and relationship with parents and other peers can be shaped by the type of content they watch on electronic media. On the other hand, any audience, whether they are children or young and old adult, can be impacted by violent TV programs and movies where aggressive behavior, attitude, and desensitization is presented.

Because of this, it is important to remember that the content should not initiate any negative target attitude or behavior instead of any positive changes[5].

Some suggestions for policy and practice for reducing the risks from content can include a media campaign, content- code rating implementation rather than age-based rating and single rating system rather than a multitude. Often a tendency in the Bangladesh media industry can be seen to simply ignore and eliminate a problematic issue rather than going into the root of the problem and solve it.

If movies showing violence to create a negative impression on the audience, then it is not the only solution to stop showing or making such movies.

Instead, the movie content could be redesigned based on different contexts and stories that would not create bad impact on the audience.

For example, when audiences in Bangladesh like to watch foreign country's satellite TV program and bring addiction and other adverse issues in their life and family, policy makers and concerned people in the society recommend banning those TV channels. This cannot be the solution to the real problem instead, professionals should focus on the core problem-creating competitive content to divert audiences from foreign TV channels.

This is why game designers do not stop designing action games or TV series do not stop showing fighting or crime instead they work on improving the context and message through their content so that adverse effects can be reduced and the audience can learn positive things from these media contents.

With a rapid move towards the social platform, the associated risks related to the content also took a new shift. This is because the human behavior has taken a fast shift, but parallel to this our ethical and legal values have not yet grabbed the primary shift[6].

The amount of content uploaded in social space daily is enormous, but copyright issues are still at huge risk in social platforms[6].

People use copyrighted content from the cyber world without permission and not much is happening yet about that. Ethical issues like taking pictures in public places and posting them as social media content are happening randomly, although before photographers needed to ask permission to take photos like this[6].

People use their personal account to communicate work-related information, post photos linking with employers and are not caring enough to stop data leakage and data theft from mobile devices.

Important to note that only audio or visual content may not be the type of content in electronic media that can initiate risks. Issues regarding how an anchor is presenting content and discussing with the audience and guests can also shape audience perception and behavior.

If a presenter just does talk shows for the sake of doing it without focusing on the main essence of it, then there is a high risk that the audience can misinterpret the message given through the program. Imagine a talk show discussion on environmental issues, giving an incorrect message to its audience and what kind of consequence that would produce.

On the other hand, an active presenter can make a boring topic interesting and make people interested in learning things which they were otherwise not interested to know about.

In conclusion, there exist media contents that are aggressive to have a negative impact on the audience. There are issues like bullying, harassment and peer-to-peer malicious communication in the online world.

However, the media content today are somehow regulated, which I believe do not function properly, or at least will need modification in the very near future. With all these things, it is still possible to state that these issues are risks only, instead of proven fact to be inevitable harm to the audience which is why they need to be taken care now.

Collecting more data on these issues and conducting in-depth research can help us understand the real problem to reduce the different risks associated with media content.

For Bangladesh these dangers are more vulnerable due to the socioeconomic and cultural causes and media organizations and professionals should already take these matters into serious attention.

CHAPTER

ECONOMIC EXTENSION

" There can be economy only where there is efficiency. "

-Benjamin Disraeli-

So far in this book we have seen the modern audience and their status and how new psychological analysis and method can help us understanding them better.

Then we have seen how this success knowledge can be brought forward for the improvement of existing content or to generate quality content. Now it is time to see what will happen if all these can occur successfully.

Of course, it will lead towards creating new competition, new market opportunities towards economic success. Similarly, failing to do this would impact negatively on the economics of the media organization. So in this Chapter, I will introduce different issues related to the electronic media and its impact on the economics of an organization and ultimately to the overall economy of the media business.

Mass media work like a catalyst for economic influence. Effects of media on economics have long been studied and are nothing new. Many theories like media agenda setting, priming, framing, and cultural theory supports the idea that mass media have a significant impact on the economy, whereas economic theories analyzed sentiments of consumers for understanding the impact of fluctuations in the economy.

However, what is interesting to explore in this respect, I believe is, how the functions and different concepts of media create impact on economics.

At the present time people spend more time online than they sleep and how does their internet use and habit impact on the economy can be something interesting to discuss, for example. Understanding things like this can help organizations improving their strategies or business model for the pathway of productivity.

Also, it is important to get insights about the structure of the organization to understand what kind of content is produced by them making money. More interestingly, digital media can offer more significant opportunities to the developing countries than in the established markets[1]. In this respect, understanding the impact of media on the economic growth of Bangladesh is crucial too. Since, according to the World Bank, Bangladeshi economy is holding a macroeconomic stability and moving forward regardless of political issues and global volatility.

Since we are living in a digital age and a digital and information technology revolution has already taken place in Bangladesh society, demonstrating the existence of media everywhere, it is apparent that improve content generation would mean new business opportunities in a country where economics is boosting up every day. This Chapter will discuss the present scopes of economics in the media business, its drawbacks, and remedies.

Digital media economics can be seen as an attention-grabbing and significant aspect of the media business that is often ignored during the planning phase of content generation. With the power of the internet, the content broadcasting concept has taken a different shift and its impact on economics is important to perceive and use by the professionals.

This Chapter will highlight the context of Bangladesh and its potentials for enhancing the digital media economics for the future and will propose steps on how to adopt those features. What could be the effective guidelines for taking expert experiences from in-house contents to a successful business scenario?

Since established market that has long experience in using digital media see the potentials of media and its impact on economic on the downside[1] it is also important to analyze the different risks associated. For instance, how do work and private life boundary impact on individual's connection with media and thereby on economics?

How could the internet be used more in Bangladesh society to take its maximum potential for the economic success of electronic media? Are there any ways the audience can participate in the content generation and then earn revenues? What should be the business strategies for the foreign audiences? Are there any agile, cost-effective models that media professionals can use within the context of Bangladesh society to restructure their existing strategies for economic success in the media business? It is the role of this Chapter to discuss these issues within the context of media industries in Bangladesh and their economic development.

While digital media can bring both benefits and risks depending on the way it is being used, we will primarily be focusing on the positive use of digital media towards understanding the impact of economic expansion. Therefore, at first in this respect, it is important to get a clear concept of what digital media economics is and how can we be benefited from this concept within the context of Bangladesh.

DIGITAL MEDIA ECONOMICS

Digital media is a type of thing that we consume every day without paying for them fully using money instead we spend time with them. Supply in the media industry has grown enormously, but demand stays the same. Sitting in a digital world we thus feel this industry is not expanding like any other high-growth industry.

However, in practice, it is a far bigger thing than it seems like. Digital news revenue, digital advertising spending, broadcast advertising revenue, network TV, internet TV, on demand TV, social media broadcasting, etc. are some of the catchy phenomena to indicate what is happening with this industry at present. The economy is related to media industry there is no doubt about it. What is important and I am going to focus in this section on some key properties of digital media economics study so that we can proceed in the next sections with this knowledge.

Over the last two decades, media economics became an individual field of study combining the study of both media and communication with the economic principles and their application in an organization management[3]. The term media economics is used "to refer to the business operations and financial activities of firms producing and selling output into the various media industries"[3].

Economics gives us answers about what, how and whom-what is produced, how is produced and for whom. When these questions are leading towards media industries and dealing with digital media, then this field of study could be titled to be digital media economics.

Digital technology has reduced production costs and new technologies are becoming cheaper for general consumers to use. This in return is changing people's behavior of accessing media content which impacts on the way content is generated and delivered. Organization and their productivity now thus depend on different parameters and digital media economics studies these kinds of issues.

———— ♦ ————

The economic potentials of digital media are huge and for a country like Bangladesh where new media and mobile technology boom is happening now, it is important to conduct a complex economic analysis of the increased productivity of the media organizations. It is possible to classify the impacts of technology and the electronic media development based on that in Bangladesh on defining the role of modern economics. The business environment in the media is highly competitive and rapidly changing. Audiences are demanding and more knowledgeable and concerned than ever before. Because of them and other rapid organizational competition business strategies are always on the go.

So to compete in such an environment, it is creativity that pays off. Creativity-driven entrepreneurship is the key to running the ever fast changing media business in Bangladesh for economic success.

Besides ICT boom and a massive increase in internet use has defined the process of globalization in Bangladesh in recent times, which plays a major role in the economic development too. In terms of content generation, outputs have a short life cycle and services offered by media organizations are volatile because audiences are driving the whole business model as it seems now and they drive the economy, therefore.

These addressed factors will now be used as my point of departure to discuss various aspects of economic expansions and scopes within the context of Bangladesh electronic media industries.

———————— • ————————

A NEW ROAD MAP

While audiences as the consumer of TV view it as a source of entertainment there are big economies involved in program creation and marketing. With the rapid change of technology and a shift in the audience thinking television as a mean of electronic media is also changing its guidelines to increase productivity for the media organizations.

I in this section will be discussing such guidelines. In this section, some suggestions are narrated and structured for increasing the productivity of media organizations, according to the requirement of modern audiences within the context of Bangladesh. During the course of writing this book in Bangladesh, we have total 28 TV channels. The competition in the TV market has increased during the past decade.

The competition of distribution of technology and expanding the market for paying the cost while competing with others are the two challenges that television broadcaster's face in terms of choosing the structure[3, 4]. In this respect, I believe a lot of TV channels in Bangladesh at present focus on vertical integration.

TV channels there, try to produce content and program that are market specific (at least they believe it is) and by that try to satisfy the common need of the audiences. However, their focus should be given more into the horizontal integration to generate content that can be related to each other. I will explain with examples here why. For example, a TV channel in Bangladesh is very famous for producing programs focusing on politics. They create quality talk shows and use reputed presenters, bring important political figures in their program to initiate constructive discussions.

The channel also has a lot of other programs that reflect the politics of Bangladesh and they are quite successful in producing this. In this way, the TV channel tries to satisfy a common need for the audiences- politics.

But for many audiences who are not interested in politics and prefer entertainment instead of heavy discussions of politics, they fail to get attracted to watch this channel. It would be wise for that TV channel to create other contents that could provide entertainment for other focused audiences, but still maintaining a relationship with their theme-politics. This way horizontal and vertical integration can be balanced for increased productivity.

It is noticeably visible in the Bangladesh media industry that organization's policy is either horizontal or vertical and still they are not successful in such integration since it is difficult and costly to get the most out from such integration.

Therefore a balance between these two types of integration would be feasible for Bangladesh media organizations. Content production can be positively and negatively affected by the vertical and horizontal integration. We can see the way programs were created even 5 years back are not the same way it is done now in Bangladesh TV channels. What it needs now is a balance between the different strategies in a content generation with respect to organization's economic policy and that can result in more strong content to capture audience interest.

One of the important aspects of media success in terms of economy is highly related to the issues of marketing. Some strategies of marketing can be worth discussing here, therefore. For media industry, even though focusing locally is the primary concern, it would be desirable to think globally[2]. After all, it is the global market pressure that sets up the framework and parameters for the local market.

Like I have discussed previously, Bangladesh has the potential and competence like other developed nation and it would be wiser to use a collaborative approach to understanding the local market with the help of an international team. The internet and social media can be a powerful tool in this respect and it would be important to track and adjust things that happen in real time. Getting invaluable insights from the other different ranges on the market can only help our media organizations prosper and be more economically productive.

The concept of global marketing can be subtle sometimes, but for media organizations that are working 24 hours, it is not a complex issue intended for the consistent benefits of their organization.

Another issue I want to point out here is the concept of media sustainability. Our media should be sustainable for proper development of the society and establishment of democracy[2]. I believe while a lot of developing nations do not bother about these issues for their media, it is extremely important for Bangladesh society. Our TV channels in Bangladesh should focus on earning from different sources and not only by sales and advertising.

They should also focus on cost reduction through promoting shared resources[2]. For sustainability in our media, the infrastructure also needs a change so that the public can access the media from various sources. If different TV channels could think of creating their content that could fit in the most dominating platform of today, the mobile phone, then it would work towards achieving sustainability using media design. This, in turn, will create a media that is economically sustainable too. Now to initiate this it is important to start assessing the capacity of our existing media. That way fair and balanced coverage of news and information can be possible through content generations by the media organization since it is after all the services for the public that the contents are all about.

It is no doubt to realize the fact at first place from a new roadmap perspective for economic success in Bangladesh media industry that we cannot compromise democracy and human rights.

The economic success for a media organization parallel to the new technology and increased audience demand can happen with the proper regulatory environment and the right professional competence in the organization for creating a sustainable economic basis for the organization. In this respect, culture should not a constraint and we need to remember that in this globalization era, it is possible for small organizations to think big which can create options for new production and thereby new markets.

———— • ————

POTENTIALS OF INTERNET

The internet has recently played a huge role in Bangladesh in triggering the process of digitization. Because of the internet apart from the communication issues different research, teaching and learning process became faster and easier[5].

The internet has in many ways played a major role as a transformer towards economic growth and success since the internet changes the way we work or even socialize[5]. However, we still are at the primary stage of using the internet and the best of the internet is yet to come.

The future massive expansion of the internet will simply show its impact more and more on the economic growth of nations and organizations.

The challenge now for Bangladesh is to take the most out of the strengths of the internet and use it in the right way. We are in the era of globalization and electronic media development in Bangladesh should compete globally as I have previously discussed in different sections of this book.

Now the world economy has undergone a global financial crisis for which the organizations and government face a huge challenge to innovate like never before and in this respect, we should not forget the enormous potentials of the internet economy that has already been brought to all nations and will continue to boost growth[5]. Thus, in Bangladesh, the policy makers, and the government should realize this potential and allow opening different opportunities for the professionals to use the internet in different possible ways in our life. However, the focus of this section is to discuss the role of the internet in driving economic growth within the context of electronic media development in Bangladesh.

In developed countries, the internet has not used the way it is used in Bangladesh, at least at present. What is important is to realize who are the beneficial in this respect since developed countries are using the internet in a different way?

Obviously, the organizations and large enterprises have benefited no doubt about it. But it is actually the consumers and different entrepreneurs who are the big winners because of such practice of internet. For media organization, this can be a trump card to increase their productivity and expand their economy.

Can organizations use the internet away so that the audiences become the big winners in Bangladesh?

I am sure all it needs is an alternation of the way of thinking and then it is possible to act on this question with success. But why this is not happening?

The government and policy makers in Bangladesh are not embracing this fact that is why. Now, I am not focusing here the role of government on expanding the availability of internet from urban to rural areas, to every corner of Bangladesh, in the hand of every possible population regardless of their ability and so on. Here I am pointing out about regulation, policy, creating value, working on dynamic, diversified supply chain and dealing with big data and analyze them for better decision making.

As an example, let's consider electronic media content generation issue. Media organizations in Bangladesh now have the ability to collect audience viewpoint through the internet and create big data sets over time. Are they doing it at present? No. The big data collection is at most, limited to issues related to government, bank, large enterprises dealing with health and education[5], but not so much in private sectors. If a TV channel, for example, would collect such data and then analyze the data set with some sophisticated algorithm then the professionals would get much more insight than they are getting now about audience perception. Now, you can imagine yourself if all media organizations in Bangladesh start practicing this creatively and effectively, then what would be the captured potential value of the market in a year?

Another interesting aspect is Internet of Things (IoT) where physical objects of everyday life around us become part of an information system by capturing and communicating information[5]. How much effort at present the media professionals in Bangladesh give to connect things? Their connectivity is limited to the live broadcast of reporting and providing the ability to remotely connect with people for running talk shows. Proper connectivity even in the virtual world is often limited.

Many organizations just use their ability to connect differently as a marketing strength with other competitors and in practice is not even using the possibilities. With the proper use of the Internet of Things live reporting and talk shows can be transferred in a different taste and quality for the audiences, experienced by them like never before. What this would do at the end is to increase efficiency while adding new capabilities to the program resulting novel business models for the organizations.

On the other hand, traditional media organization models can be thought from the viewpoint of the social network model. I believe a fundamental shift will take place in the very near future regarding how individuals organize themselves in multifaceted networks[5]. The Internet has the power for developing a new market, give services, allow participation and then mainstream this factors[5]. So collaboration can take a different form if the organizational model is shifted from the traditional to network type. Let's say for a TV channel the organizational model is completely their customized social media based. The network would include the expertise of the organization, their customers, stakeholders and even previous employees. Imagine then how effective the collaboration work would be while dealing with issues like the audience, their psychology or content? How fast accomplishing a complex, specialized project would then be? You sure can think again the economic value of such practice.

So the challenge now is how to motivate media organizations to use the internet differently and in this respect what could be the triggers? It is not as simple as going to individuals and tells them how to use the internet in different ways instead we should work on supplementary issues that would trigger the organization's internet use pattern. Some of such triggers are discussed below:

Intensification of Competition

The market in the Bangladesh media sector is not open. In a closed market, expecting productivity increase is difficult. If competition is increased the media organizations would then create more innovative content.

In Bangladesh, the competition is still within the scope of personal benefits instead of improvement of the public and society. Opening up the market can trigger real competition when media organization can use the internet in different ways for contributing the growth. If a TV channel starts showing their ability to use the internet differently in a program, then another TV channel will try to do something else with the internet for competing with the other. Organizations in that way can gain market share and create attractive contents and services for the audiences.

Work on Inspiring Innovation

Can competition trigger innovation? Or does it need proper environment? Can competition create the proper environment then? What does environment mean from electronic media, internet and economics context?

I believe if policy makers give effort towards such complex thought, innovation would be triggered automatically. Unfortunately, too little emphasis even close to these is given in Bangladesh media at present. Do the media organizations in Bangladesh have proper support for research, required capital, collaboration to academic world? These things trigger creating the appropriate environment. I add a personal experience here as an example.

The first private TV channel in Bangladesh in the year 2000 where I worked as a presenter made sure to have access to many of these parameters which are why they could innovate something unique at that time.

Audiences accepted the channel like anything; they have accepted that channel like they would never ever accept any other new TV channels in Bangladesh. With respect to the internet, it is similarly important to create an environment that can help to capture internet-related growth for the media organization.

However, it is important to understand the preliminary internet based design for the organization is needed at first place for such innovation to think about.

Develop Individual Economic Value

Media organizations in Bangladesh usually recruit people that they believe has the right competence in serving their organization. But how do they measure this? It is not possible to measure individuals just by looking at their professional profile. Every individual capability can be converted to an economic value.

The internet is a great resource for organizations to learn about the human values of their employees. The internet can be used for attracting competitive employees into the organization. It can be very effective for new companies. Media organization of today should get benefited by this.

Bangladesh government can play a huge role in creating such

internet-related human capital. As an example, different organizations in the USA can be mentioned here who are well known for hunting talents from around the world using this method.

That way they continue doing their own innovation and positively impact on the economy.

A considerable number of populations of Bangladesh are now living in overseas and the rate of moving to a foreign country is gradually increasing. A lot of talents are serving organizations in other countries while they still could be a great resource for the home country if internet based human capital could be developed. The media industry in this respect, especially, can be highly benefited from this concept.

As discussed earlier, it is possible to create a network structure of the organization instead of the traditional one, where foreign experts can also be a part of the extended network for increasing the productivity of an organization.

Sharing and Improving Structure

Building the proper infrastructure is a must for increasing growth and is one of the problems with Bangladesh as I have already mentioned. It is not about building a solid infrastructure of the internet for the whole country and become productive, instead, it is a continuous process too.

Technology is changing rapidly. Internet infrastructure that was regulated in the year 2000 in Bangladesh for example, cannot be same now, which unfortunately is the case now. Like

I have mentioned the prospects of big data, Internet of Things and a network model of organization the infrastructure should be redesigned based on these concepts, for example. The telecommunication revolution happened in the last 15 years in Bangladesh and maybe internet infrastructure was feasible to give greater importance to telecommunication sector based on which a lot of new innovative development has taken place.

Now the media boom has occurred and the internet infrastructure should be expanded to allow innovation happen in media fields by engaging more users into the process. Again, the policy makers and government in Bangladesh should really play the key card in this respect.

———— • ————

NEW BUSINESS MODEL

We represent an organization in an abstract manner with the help of a business model. Since the economic growth of media organizations can be seen from a different angle due to the advancement of technology and audience competence, a few words on the characteristics of a new business model for the electronic media organizations is worthy here.

Discussing the basic business model of electronic media can be started with advertising which acts as the fuel for driving the economics of broadcast television where the advertising revenue sources are influenced by different cynical events[3].

The unusual nature of economics related to broadcast is dealing with dual market and two products-consumers watching the TV and advertisers interested in the audiences[3]. Thus, understanding the customers is the center of a traditional business model for an electronic media organization.

The core question asked in this standard model is what

values are created for the customer which also can mean what it actually means in practice to create value for customers[6]. But now the paradigm of technology driven economics is here, which is shifting the old media business model. But what is needed to understand is that technology cannot alone make changes happen instead we need to change the business model so that the advantages of technology can be taken into practice for economic boost ups.

For media organizations as I have discussed earlier, through content generation values are created and delivered to the audiences through whom values are then again captured too.

So if we discuss the nine principle segments of a business model[7] within the context of a new audience, new content and ongoing technological shifts we may end up getting a different business model given that the central focus of the model would still remain to be value creation for the audiences.

I will discuss different segments of a business model below within the context of Bangladesh and based on the ideas and concepts introduced and discussed in the previous Chapters in this book.

For whom do we create value and how do we understand who are the important customers is a complex question. Due to the demographic and socioeconomic classification audiences are classified in Bangladesh in different groups. Technology centered and totally illiterate audiences exist in Bangladesh and specifying one single group of customer is delicate, therefore.

It is thus wiser to generate content and thereby values for the different categories of audiences. Identifying most important customers can be simplified by grouping them into different categories based on different variables like economic state, educational background, and age etc.

Next the proposition of values is what the organizations need to think. What values should organizations deliver to its client would depend on the categories of the client. Identifying customer's problem would be easier by categorizing them and then it becomes easier to satisfy the need of specific groups of customer.

Media organizations can identify these and according to the result, can customize their content generation strategies for delivering appropriate values to the right audiences.

The next phase is the channel segment where it is important to select the most feasible channels through which information can be transformed to the clients. There comes the issue of mobile content, social media application and traditional TV program content delivery. It is extremely important to identify which channels work best, which channels can be integrated and which one is cost effective for the organization. Also, selection of proper channel would depend upon the ability of the customer integration too.

———— ♦ ————

Connecting with the customers brings us to the phase to serving them. Organizations should be careful in analyzing what kind of connectivity and relationship different customer segments identified earlier would allow the organizations to maintain. If there are any existing relationships, then organizations need to evaluate cost-effectiveness of them and find relationships with the other part of the business model.

How audiences are attracted to get a hook to the content produced by media organizations and what makes them like the content and for which values, is the next thing to look for. The benefits of these should be compared with the total benefits earned by the organizations in their business model.

Identifying the proper values that satisfied customers can be benefited from will trigger improved content generation for the organizations.Identifying the important resources, activities, and partners required for value proposition is the next stage.

An organization can use their distribution channels or customer relationship or combine them and other different resources together to achieve success in this. It is likely that value proposition in one channel cannot be as same as if it is practiced through another channel.

Due to the versatile nature of audiences and their taste selecting the key resources are important.

Finally, analysis of the cost that is most important in the business model for the organization comes into action.

Maybe some key activities or resources selected earlier are expensive and will increase the overall cost of the business model. Maybe generating content in one way is more feasible than the other way. Maybe it is optimal to outsource and crowdsource some contents than to develop than inside the organization.

Maybe practicing open innovation is more practical for value added content creation for media organizations. All these issues need in-depth consideration and analysis.

In Bangladesh media business context, it is important to understanding the dual nature of media economics-policymakers need to realize that it is about selling programs and also selling the audience who watch the program. Existing audience evaluation methods are not capable of going with the pace of electronic media movement in Bangladesh.

Even though most media behavior can be explained by

economics, it is crucial to realize that there is a potential danger resulting degradation of the originality and quality in the content generation since the Bangladesh media environment is increasingly fragmented and autonomous where it is going to be more and more difficult to monitor audiences.

It is, therefore, important to analyze audiences through the eyes of economics and in this respect dealing with the proper business model is vital for the media organizations.

There exist several business models that organizations use or follow which they believe is appropriate for them. For Bangladesh electronic media organizations this issue is more critical than adapting an existing business model.

I believe it would be ideal to go through these nine segments as I have discussed here and then formulate customized structured business model that can be a fit for the appropriate purpose for a media organization while the society deals with complex political, economic and digital divide issues in a country.

For an example, just analyzing the impact of internet only, with each of the discussed nine segments of business model would result in complex enough results to shape the business model of a media organization since they are becoming more complex and their nature of the business to survive in the competitive market is becoming tougher. It would probably be desirable to identify a hybrid business model for satisfactory revenue generation for today's complex media organizations-especially in Bangladesh.

———— ♦ ————

A SHIFT TOWARDS ECONOMIC SUCCESS

With all the important aspects of media economics in the context of Bangladesh discussed so far, what matters, in the end, is how we can adapt a positive shift towards the economic success of our present state of the media industry. The global digital revolution has created a massive change in the sales and marketing, especially for the small to medium organizations.

It is a challenge to move towards successful economic growth for the holistic economic success of an organization. In this section, I will write down some of the suggestions to make this process smooth. However, the followings are just suggestions and not any method.

Self-Dependency

Organizations should focus on the true fact that they are responsible for creating their own problem and they need to solve it.

They need to fix their goal and achieve it by themselves apparently. But then again if every individual by an organization think this way that they need to achieve their own goal and be responsible for their own acts a combinatorial result will boost the economic productivity of the organization.

Being positive and trusting on oneself always will result a brighter future.

Dealing with different circumstances, even though they are a disaster can be one of the important keys to make an organization successful in the long run.

Active Involvement

Media organizations need to give more efforts for the success in Bangladesh. There are many factors organization management needs to deal with rather than content creation or audience satisfaction. Organizations need to give more effort for finding new ways to get more done in a shorter period of time. Organizations can plan to run their workflow in an improved way, for example, and use new technology for increasing their productivity.

Active involvement in a way to make an organization separated from others is what will matter in the future economic race. For example, journalists focusing on economics should actively collaborate and involve themselves with academic economists.

On the other hand, the academics also may have something to learn from the journalists. This type of active involvement is not visible in Bangladesh society at present since there are other issues that are preventing individuals from these to happen. However, online engagement can help in this respect and involvement can be more active by maintaining user privacy in a different way.

Legalization Issues

Many different unnecessary standards set by the industry can be a hinder for media organizations to move forward. Legalization issues are an issue, especially in a country like Bangladesh.

There are laws that are unfair and government and

policymakers should open their mind up regarding these.

There should not be any law that can prevent the country's media boost while other country's TV channels can take the market from the local audience and this should be considered with great caution.

Trigger Innovations

As discussed earlier in different sections of this book, innovation is the start-up fuel for any economic growth. For Bangladesh and its media industry, innovative idea generation and implementation is the key through which the future nation will build upon.

The policies of the country should be pursued accordingly to encourage innovation that the next generation can carry with high prosperity. New innovative idea generation for creating cutting edge content for the TV channels can initiate this step easily since it will not cost extra to do such because of the existing setup.

Focusing on The Web

The web has unlimited opportunities and it is the digital kingdom for us at present where we can reflect our thoughts the way we want. It is very important to realize the critical importance of having and maintaining a website for media organizations.

Unfortunately, present scenarios in Bangladesh regarding this is that many TV channels just have a website which is not even being updated regularly, that is to say, they just started a website for the sake of showing the world that they have a website. But, for TV channels a website can be a powerful tool where the organization can show their story, can connect with different companies and create a huge impression to the existing and new potential customers. Website design should also focus on user friendliness and useful in terms of engaging with customers.

Listening to the Social World

Social computing has enormous power, but how many TV channels and media organization truly utilize this in Bangladesh can be realized easily once we analyze their status in the social media world. While it is important to have an own company website, it is equally important now to haves social space in the cyber world.

The social media use for media organizations should be strategic and not only just be limited within the scope of sharing and liking.

That way it will be possible for organizations to get a holistic picture of what is going on in the industry, where do they need to work on, what is their relationship with their clients and how things get triggered online by the influence of people in charge and so on. Sharing appropriate content for the target audiences to attract them can be key through social media.

Understanding these would in return impact on the realizing competitors and their relationships with the clients for generating new business thoughts leading towards improved productivity.

Character on Mobile

People accessing the web using mobile devices are increasing enormously and this trend is highly visible in

Bangladesh due to the new media, the internet, and mobile technology boom that have happened in recent times.

A vast number of traffic on the internet thus comes from the mobile devices. The purpose of mobile phones, for example, is not anymore limited to talk or communicate via text only. It is thus simply foolish to ignore mobile technology for the media organizations at present.

Users are becoming more and more tech savvy due to the massive growth of mobile devices like smartphones and tablets which are why this forces us to focus on mobile optimized content generation.

Media organizations should focus on creating mobile friendly content, website that can be easier for the mobile devices to consume and respond. In a more advanced way, an organization can be a separate branch that can develop its own mobile strategy to deal with a focused group of clients. Why would audiences come to see the content of one TV channel and not another one?

Organizations dealing with media content generation in Bangladesh should thus engage themselves to determine how to add value to their content and method of distribution so that people are interested to see their content. Focusing mobile technology is a key in achieving this at present era.

There should thus be multiple ways to attract clients in the content generated by media organizations and in this respect alone mobile technology will be playing a massive role in coming future.

Commitment Building

Let's imagine a TV channel has their own website that they

maintain regularly and updates the content, they have their own pages on different social media and it is possible for online users to find about the company very easily.

Now how would doing all these simply will increase productivity if users hit the page and leave? What is needed then is to attract clients. One way to do is creating a community where members have similar interest and choice. Using RSS, email, like, follow, share can be a powerful tactic in this situation to make a company leading other competitors. However, the process of success through this may not be instantaneous since the majority population of Bangladesh still does not access the internet, but this trend is expanding fast and over time it will be possible to build a strong potential community to earn trust and build commitment to the clients for their media organizations.

Increase Visibility

Content is not for one-time view or use only. If content can be reused and rebuild based on previous information that was published then the visibility of the content along with its organization would take place.

Existing content can also be extended and that would initiate truly sustainable media development.

For instance, the website content of a TV channel can be reused to create a presentation, a video for the social world, or an article on their blog.

By practicing such organizations would be able to show that they can be multifaceted and that they have diversity in a content generation which would attract more consumers in the long run.

This way content should be upcycling and then productivity should boost for the organizations. Also, using social media optimally can be another great way to make organizations more visible to the world.

Dealing with Content

It is after all the content that is designed for the audiences that assess the success of a media organization.

In today's technology and the internet driven world, it is thus not enough to produce content for TV only instead the organizations should focus on more dynamic content generation because the internet and personal computer together have created a new era in the entertainment business.

That way it would be possible to let the world know what this organization is capable of doing, what kind of problem they are addressing and why they are important and so on. It is all about telling the story of what organizations are capable of doing and a success in telling good stories will attract a positive customer response. Just telling the story via TV program is going to be weaker and weaker and different other formats of the program will get priority.

This is highly connected with mobile technology too. Users soon will not have enough time or patience to see their favorite content on TV when the channel is broadcasting them, instead, they would like to see the content whenever they want, wherever they are. Are our TV channels ready for this?

Can we access any TV program anytime we want from our mobile device or organization's website? Not at this moment, according to my honest judgment.

This issue is critical for defining the economic success for future media organizations. Also allowing individuals to be active in content creation is another important issue that digital media has initiated and should be considered by organizations for their improved productivity.

CHAPTER

DIGITAL SOCIAL REVOLUTION

" Yesterday is not ours to recover, but tomorrow is ours
to win or lose. "

-Lyndon B. Johnson-

The concluding Chapter of this book will address the
issues with politics and policy making for the media
business in Bangladesh and the challenges these would
create for the future generations. I started exploring the factors
of what is happening to our TV through the analysis of
audiences.

Then we looked into the advance notions of audience
psychology. After that, we saw how quality content can be
generated based on the knowledge we gather from the audience
and their perception.

Later we saw how new economic extensions and
opportunities can be triggered and taken into consideration for
the media organization. Now, finally, it is important, to sum up
all these aspects to address the digital social revolution that will
be further triggered in Bangladesh is going to be the ultimate
focus of this Chapter since a massive opening towards a digital
revolution is indicated with the issues discussed so far.

It is difficult to draw a definitive conclusion about the digital revolution and international development, but it should not cause us to be timid with our questions[4]. What needs to be done to prepare us for such a revolution in Bangladesh?

Why do people in Bangladesh need to approve and be ready for such adoption? How do we do it? What could be the advantages and disadvantages for the future generations for such alteration?

What lessons can we learn from other cultures and countries and imply them into the development of electronic media in Bangladesh? Why we are not being able to take full potential of such revolution yet and how can we overcome that?

How can politics be overlooked in the development of electronic media in Bangladesh? How can public awareness take a different shape in the post digital revolution?

How to effectively use and apply social media as a tool for the success of these purposes? How to focus on the mass population of Bangladesh that is mostly living in the rural areas and takes advantage from these audiences? What policymakers should do in these respects? This Chapter will briefly discuss these.

The root of innovation that has mainly impacted in Bangladesh society for a digital revolution is the reduction of price in the personal computer and mobile technology, affordable internet cost and outsourcing business together with start-up cultures. However, it is important to realize like I have discussed before that improved infrastructure is needed to get the most out of these phenomena.

To create improved infrastructure it requires different authoritative peoples in charge to take the right decision at the right time. The role of politicians is one of the preliminary issues of media developments in Bangladesh. Again, politicians and their role are not always assessed in Bangladesh based on the criteria of someone being elected to serve the government by the public voting instead politician there can also mean people with authorization and ability to make things happen.

A concrete discussion of the political paradigm and policy-making issues in Bangladesh within the context of media development is, therefore, important at first place and is presented below.

——— • ———

POLITICAL PARADIGM

Politics is probably the most discussed issues for the people in Bangladesh. Political instability has been a natural practice in Bangladesh for years. However, it is the government that has often taken breakthrough decisions in terms of expanding the scopes in the electronic media business in Bangladesh.

It is quite common that a ruling government often issues transmission license for new TV channels to a set of organizations while some other potential organizations do not get accepted during the rule of that specific government. In turn, if another government comes in power, then they issue license for their preferred organizations.

The government also has regulations on the internet, mobile and print media policy along with laws for the cyber and social world on the internet. While all these things are accepted, I believe, for a real social change and the digital revolution to take place, and continue with its success, the government and politicians should play the key role in Bangladesh.

As a simple example, innovative content and ideas can be

generated by different private TV channels in Bangladesh but how about if the government there does not create an optimal environment for these things to take place for real?

Thus, the transformation of the changes in the media can happen with the proper role played by the government.

For instance, more populations in Bangladesh are and will be using mobile devices and they soon would like to see their favorite TV channel contents while they are on public transport for example.

If the government creates a specific rule about this issue, then it is not going to be materialized and the government can also feel the impact on such decision both negative and positive ways. A strict decision in the privacy of cyber world by the government, on the other hand, can be appreciated by the people.

When the technological revolution happens, it does not only impact on a specific set of technology, rather it influences the economy, it changes the identity of individuals while issues like security and sustainability are also affected.

The government in Bangladesh should be thinking more holistically about this crucial point. When someone wants a policy or regulation alternation for the electronic media business, it may not be an isolated field of interest that would get benefited through the new policy.

The government must think that there are other systems that are connected with this electronic media business issues that impact on the social, cultural and economic system of the country.

Supervisory authorities like the government in Bangladesh should thus never forget to consider the importance of "the whole eco-system[1]" connected with each other for the progress of the whole nation.

———— • ————

POLICYMAKING

Media set agenda for policy makers and this effect is highly significant. Decision making can be influenced and triggered by the strength of, media which makes a media act as a practical source of power.

But if policy makers want to contribute to media development, they should not be biased by the agenda that any existing media set up for them, instead, they need to be open towards forming new policies for the organization.

A successful policy-making can be a talent that needs, combining different skills where policy maker works as a funnel to gain more information and reduce and extract them later in the form of policies for promoting a preferred course of action. So the process of policy formation should take place in a caring way in a media organization since media deliver an important message to the mass populations.

This issue is very important for Bangladesh media industries where policy makers are often biased or like to go with the traditional flow. Sometimes they are influenced by politics and politicians too. In this respect, it is crucial that these policy makers engage themselves in the consultation process.

It is also important for them to become a good listener and combine these characteristics with their own expertise. They also need to combine other methods like survey, statistical analysis, monitor events etc. for better decision making. Participating online discussion forums can also give them new insights about what is important for them to take a decision on. Another important thing is to collaborate with different experts from outside the own organization.

Consulting with academics and government officials can help them gain new insights on different topics that they may not be an expert in.

The policy making process is supported by policy analyst, policy makers, and politicians. Regarding the success of electronic media in Bangladesh, policymakers should be supported by different policy analysts who can identify and prioritize necessary policy issues.

They need to work on reviewing the existing government policy based on the objectives and interests of the media sector. For this, they need to identify existing policies and their consequences for the media business. Then they need to analyze and identify if new policies are developed and implemented what would be the direct and indirect consequences of them and what kind of risks will be associated and through this policy makers can progress towards the objectives of the media sector through their competence.

Sometimes one or two policies may not be appropriate for achieving a target objective and a set or group of policies in the form of a policy package needs to be developed for the effectiveness of the identified goal. Policymakers thus need to involve themselves to advocate these viable policy packages in a clear, brief and persuasive way.

This way policy analysis can help policy makers to take difficult decisions in complex situations. While policymakers can understand issues to make good decisions, policy analysts can convey this understanding quickly. Important here to realize is that politicians cannot be ignored during the formulation of policies that are implementable.

Policy makers can challenge the real world by their policy with an aim to affect it, but then again, it is useless to propose policies that would not be accepted because of political reasons. Therefore politics and politicians are, in fact, central to policy issues. They should not be ignored or viewed as a side issue even though it may be difficult in Bangladesh context.

While technologies and its applications can contribute to boost op economy and other social advantages, people with higher authorities in the government or other experts in charge should support to make these changes materialize in Bangladesh.

Their contribution can help Bangladesh to move further stage ahead in the world of digitization. For example, there are regulations on mobile and internet policy in Bangladesh. The internet changes the way we look into policy and it is a dynamic process.

Regulatory authorities dealing with these should analyze the issues beyond communication through mobile and the internet only, instead, they should be looking into the holistic picture of the whole nation and positive impact of ICT on the Bangladesh society through mobile and the internet.

Wise decision making would be possible if this is how policy makers think. Old established policies that were developed years ago should be looked through fresh eyes for their updates that would fit in the present technology era.

For Bangladesh, the revolution of digitization has started, but it is the right decision of different policy makers that can define the future trigger and continuation of this revolution.

Proper decision making from the right policy makers can thus in the coming future decide the fact of translating different opportunities into the reality for the success of Bangladesh electronic media industries.

———————— • ————————

PUBLIC AWARENESS

Our world is becoming a global village and developing countries like Bangladesh, can no longer afford to take the back seat on the issue of media globalization and taking advantage of the technology driven media- a shift that already has started shaping people's thought there. Public awareness has a direct correlation with media coverage like many other issues.

It is, however, important to realize that public awareness about media is needed for the social change and digital revolutions in Bangladesh to continue with its success. Media covers all types of information about health, environment, and politics, but how about the media produce content about the media itself?

That is not really happening in Bangladesh at present, but it can have a massive implication on shaping people's way of thinking about electronic media and its usage.

Professionals in the media business need to educate themselves better for understanding the impact technology in electronic media and to teach them how to get benefit out of it.

A broader popular understanding of the present situation and perspectives of electronic media in Bangladesh with its proper functioning can be promoted through such education and training work to journalists and other people involved in media development in different media organizations.

Public awareness work can be taken in different forms like press conferences, article writing, interviews and roundtable discussions in the workshop or academic conference.

The information or result from such events can be shared with appropriate policy makers or government officials in Bangladesh while at the same time it is important to remember that public awareness should not be misinterpreted by the government as an advertising method instead it should be perceived as a medium to give the right persons in charge the messages for value creation in government decision makings.

A successful process of this will lead towards changing the attitudes of government officials for generating better policy for the ideal media development in Bangladesh. This change of attitude can initiate more support, more out of the box thinking and modifying laws for business.

It is the journalist who plays the major role in creating public awareness even though in developing countries they face many challenges in reporting policy issues. There are a lot of journalists in Bangladesh who did not go through any professional training and they even lack specialization for which they need to embrace more ethical values and accuracy in their reporting, learn through proper training and education if needed, which can help them gain more trust and then the government's relationship with them can become sound over time.

Sometimes media organizations for many different reasons apart from the incompetence of journalist, may not find some interesting story that would be important in creating public awareness.

Organizations in this situation can get information from the external sources if possible to get attention-grabbing and interesting stories for adding value in the content generated by the organization. The performance of a media organization can this way be increased.

Finally, it is not a responsibility of government or media organization alone, neither all blames can be put on the journalists. Officials in charge cannot expect that media will always go to them asking for information. They need to give the effort to convey important information to the media too. The TV talk show is a great way for conveying information from the professionals. Bangladesh media industry needs to focus on other aspects of life on TV talk shows so that experts in different fields can come and spread knowledge and new information to the public.

New media and electronic media issues can be one of such topic of interest.

Together all involved in the process of media development need to be enlightened on understanding and spreading the vital information about the happenings in an electronic media revolution in Bangladesh to the general audiences for their awareness so that the process can continue. Ability to sharing information on the internet is a great way to initiate this process. Since journalists can now access the internet anytime, anywhere and it is possible to self-educate themselves on any issues if they need that which will help them, creating better coverage about different subjects of interest for mass population in Bangladesh.

———— • ————

INTERNATIONALISATION

Internationalization of business is not any novel new idea and for Bangladesh media industries this can mean producing content for other countries.

The phenomena of communicating internationally have been an active interlocutor since media and information technologies play the major role in globalization process[3]. Organizations can distribute their content made in the home country across many others.

Organizations with no origin or nationality are the ultimate conceptual goal in this respect, where content generated back home will bring revenue from overseas.

Similarly, the content developed for promoting in a foreign country can include different materials for representing the local culture. Sometimes this globalization of culture is compared to a conceptual magnet because of its attractive power of research from different disciplines. It is important to remember in this fast, technology-driven globalization era that the local media business is highly affected by what is happening out there globally

But then again, at the same time in this respect, it is important not to forget the concept of regionalization. For media organizations, a key focus should be given within their own region to expand their business.

Globalization can then be fostered through this. Neighboring countries of Bangladesh have successfully practiced regionalization in their media business which is why they have been successful in capturing the regional market and their audiences. Bangladesh is yet to be successful in this aspect.

One important thing regarding this is to focus on the large population groups in Bangladesh living in the rural area.

A huge prospective audience group is out there who are often overlooked. Within the country the concept of regionalization can be practiced by looking into the diverse need of these focused group audiences and content can be generated for their focused need. This way, successful regionalization inside the country can result in a combinatorial national success which can eventually trigger regionalization outside the country.

CONVERGENCE OF NEW MEDIA

Developed and many developing countries have changed over to the digital transmission of their broadcast service. Bangladesh is yet to see this change, but it is a powerful phenomenon for media organizations.

Digital TV is not only about providing better picture quality, but there are issues like video on demand that is very important for Bangladesh audiences.

In Bangladesh, it seems now people are in the collision between old and new media, which is why the power of interaction in media producers and consumers is not yet effectively discovered for higher profitability. The convergence of different communication system along with different cultures can create new organizational and economic structure for existing media organizations.

A new role from the perspective of advertising for the audience by increasing their demand could then also be implemented. Convergence thus creates and increases competition between media organizations and can be effective in achieving higher productivity. Digital TV within the context of Bangladesh was just one given an example here, but the media convergence is not only about technology but a relation of consumer and producer of content for economic, social and political implications.

Like I have discussed earlier in this book, triggering media innovation, internationalization and convergence of media platforms, content and different services, increased access to internet and mobile technology, encouraging user-generated content for electronic media- all these can be seen through the eyes of new media convergence in Bangladesh and have enormous potential for media development and its success. For a successful continuation of the innovative digital and social revolution in Bangladesh, the media convergence issue should be taken into serious consideration for an effective production and distribution of public information content in a significant way.

---- ◆ ----

DIVERSITY AND QUALITY

Media diversity and quality issues of media content can immensely give momentum to the ongoing digital revolution in Bangladesh. Offering new opportunities for media diversity in important for the organizations in the age of technology driven media.

At present, the media landscape is pretty open and free in Bangladesh and getting opinions and ideas from multiple sources are a sign of succeeding towards a democratic society. The concept of media pluralism comes into the picture in this respect.

Pluralism in the media reflects the diversity in a general way. However, the concept can be further explained in the form of internal and external pluralism where issues like social and political diversity, media organization itself, channel, titles, contents and editorial boards etc.

In Bangladesh, media pluralism practice can trigger the ongoing social and digital revolution that was triggered using new media. Analyzing the content can assess the media diversity which is the heterogeneous characteristics of the media content.

Bangladesh media organizations should focus on assessing media diversity by looking into the reflective and open diversity analysis of the content. Ultimately the media organizations should try to work on promoting the diversity in media as it is one of the critical goals in media policy.

Diversity and market competition analysis are important for realizing the economic impact of the media. The quality of the content is another important aspect where different quality measurement methods that are appropriate for the focused group audiences in Bangladesh should be developed. Social media can affect the quality of the content in different ways too. With so much diversification of media content, quality is being redefined now.

Quality is difficult to assess in general ways rather it should be analyzed subjectively and contextually- for different audiences in different circumstances. The modern concept of emotional marketing through social media where empathic contents are made to strike the audience emotion can be a great way to change contents to be more beneficial by adding supplementary values into it.

———— • ————

SOCIAL MEDIA

By representing an enormous opportunity social media proves to be one of the most powerful and influential platforms in today's world. There are risks associated with social media along with its positive sides like broader market creation and establishing corporate citizenship for organizations.

Now, we have seen before how effective use of social media can be beneficial for electronic media organizations in Bangladesh. But to get such benefits it is important for an organization to use right professionals for balancing the positive and negative aspects of using social media in their business. So the department of IT, marketing, and finance together with HR should work together to assess the state of using social media in a media organization.

In Bangladesh, active and optimal use of social media for the media organizations is yet to take place. Policymakers of an organization can play a key role in this respect to make the right decision on how to use social media for the success of their business.

In Bangladesh mobile device and social media soon will become a standard business tool because people have accepted the interaction style with these two elements of the technology revolution.

How people in Bangladesh get news, how they start or do small business, how they meet with friends and communicate with them, what they can reveal and influence, are in recent time redefined in Bangladesh through the power of social media. People's expectation has increased already and it is always demanding for something new and unique for them to accept. Media organizations can use this demand as their business policy by generating and delivering content to be optimized for mobile devices and social media, which would create a big difference in their marketing and profitability.

But then again, it is important to remember that the flow of information in social media is not controlled. Mass media communication is facilitated by social media where anyone can contribute in adding any information they want. This challenge of social media is more than any other platform like print media, for example. For electronic media in Bangladesh to get the most out of the social media world, policy makers again can play a key role.

———— • ————

COMPUTATIONAL JOURNALISM

Computational journalism is a very modern and new evolving conception where journalism and computer science is blended together for understanding the fundamental nature of news over computer networks. By the power of algorithm and artificial intelligence this research field aims to find out the source of news and how it is consumed, which the journalist otherwise would need to do it manually and this is where computation journalism creates its values.

Often, known as the data-driven journalism, computational journalism deals with analyzing large sets of data, for producing more credible news.

Three contextual factors about computational journalism can be the availability of large data, increased online participation, and convenience of free web 2.0 applications[5]. A combination of these contexts opens up the opportunities to conduct advanced research with data sets that are open and free to use. The proper use of computational journalism can facilitate improved collaboration and co-creation opportunities between different types of a journalist like professional, citizen and even with readers[5].

There are numerous challenges involved in the process of adopting computational journalism practice in the newsroom, but crowdsourcing can already be used for practicing the process of co-reporting. In this respect, the journalists can use a web platform to collaborate with others and divide their work of producing a report.

An individual journalist can get the work done this way in a few hours that would otherwise take him or her to do a week. In Bangladesh, the concept of computational journalism has a big prospect, although it may need some time to establish this practice. In analyzing political news and, crime reporting this method can be very useful.

At present organizations like Associated Press (AP) and The Guardian are using computational journalism and it is a very interesting research field where academics are giving more effort in generating new methods. For Bangladesh media organizations, even a partial implementation or use of computational journalism concept can help them stand in the crowd and can add enormous unique business values for increasing their productivity.

As we saw in the previous Chapter that a shift of business model is desired because of the new technology and audience demand one cannot deny that the need for people to aggregate news or entertainment will go away. Future television viewers will like to control their own content and participate in generating content of their choice too, and in this respect, they will like the idea of using the power of computational journalism service to put on a big show for them. Because of this, the understanding of the electronic media's economic impact would also take a different shape in the future.

———— • ————

ARE WE PREPARED

While explaining the effects of digital revolution James Beniger[2] said that mass media and communication along with their way of digitizing happening at present has blurred the earlier differences between communication and information processing along with man and machine. He continued, "Digitization makes communications from persons to machines, between machines, and even from machines for persons as easy as it is between persons. Also blurred are the distinctions among information types: numbers, words, pictures, and sounds, and eventually taste, odors, and possibly even sensations, all might one day be stored, processed, and communicated in the same digital format".

With all these fascinating characteristics of digitization, the question still can be, are we in Bangladesh really ready or getting ready for adopting such changes within the context of electronic media development as I have discussed in this book?

That is a difficult question to answer.

In 1979 when the Sony Walkman was introduced, 200 million units were sold. It was hard to imagine for many analysts that something else could be innovated similar to Sony Walkman that would sell that much. But in 2001 Apple iPod sold 350 million units. Both Apple iPod and Sony Walkman are portable devices for music. Today we talk about digital TV, on demand TV and web-based content broadcasting. These certainly are not the best that happened to TV yet. Even though none of these three unique features of modern TV are noticeable yet in Bangladesh, other countries are thinking about advancing the TV- thinking it to be more contextual, ubiquitous and integrated so that it can be more customer focused.

The future of TV will be redefining content. There will be

ubiquitous screens dominating for content mobility. New dimensions of content will drive innovation beyond the traditional studio concept. Audiences will gain more ability to personalize and measure content. Where are we in Bangladesh, standing while all these are already happening? If we are not prepared, then it is time to act and get prepared anyways. Trends always drive the future and if we are not prepared, we will fall behind in every respect of life in Bangladesh. In today's world, the consumers are in control. Audiences are in control for the TV industry, therefore. If we are not ready to give them things that they want, then we will end up losing them.

If you like it or not, but Bangladesh is changing. Some changes are slow and not noticed easily while others are rapid and significant. A change within electronic media is one of such revolutionary change that has and is happening in Bangladesh at present.

Media professionals, policy makers, and politicians in Bangladesh need to remember one thing that- change is difficult and scary even though it almost always brings opportunities for learning new things or improve ourself[1]. There is no quick fix in the world of digital divide; money cannot solve it, writing another book will not solve it either. Proper planning and structuring realistic strategies can help. What would be wise, therefore, is to better adapt and welcome the changes instead of being afraid and try to avoid or resist it?

———— ♦ ————

CHALLENGE FOR THE FUTURE

For the media industries in Bangladesh to foster a growth that can sustain over time, are progressive and tries to include most possible peoples from the society, ultimately demands political stability in the country. Private investment in media sector should be encouraged and the government should pay attention more than now to regulate private media sectors. Decision makers and politicians in Bangladesh have learned a lot in recent decades.

But still, the success of what these people in charge have learned depends on the diverse capacity, leadership and communication ability of the selected persons to work. So what is needed is right people at the right time.

Selecting the right people to make right decisions and generate or rework useful policies for media development would result in a fair condition for the future generation in Bangladesh.

This is the eventual challenge for Bangladesh to get benefit through the power of digital electronic media completely. The future generation then will be successfully able to interact with the ecosystem of media for the success of their social relations.

It is the right time to re-balance Bangladesh society in this respect so that the transformative change through the power of electronic media becomes a reality in the future. Who in this respect should be the voice then?

Current media professionals and marginalized potential media workers in Bangladesh can start working on this issue already now since they represent the future children of Bangladesh.For taking care the challenges initiated by the new media explosion in Bangladesh it is thus important that people in today's society walk fearlessly in the path of media development. Generating lots of ideas, even though they are bad or not going to be implemented is still important for practicing constant development on an issue.

This way people can refine and shape their vision more. Similarly, it is not a problem to only imagine a vision, since working towards that imagination constantly can help people identifying their true vision.

This is very important for the rapid development of electronic media. People in Bangladesh need to care about the changes in their society that have started on the basis of technological impact. Whether it is small or big change, people need to be passionate about it and this is the primary ingredients for the success of a social revolution. They need to devote themselves to make this change to move forward since this change and revolution is and will be helping the population to a larger extent than never before. Since this will have a long-term impact in years to come in shaping the quality of life of the Bangladeshi people. Electronic media revolution has a distinctive quality where the authority in Bangladesh has already worked on and now it should be a collective movement to create similar values.

This kind of phenomena can then be an ideal example for other developing countries when they also can feel, that what has happened in Bangladesh in terms of electronic media revolution is worth copying in their society.

What do all these things that I have discussed in this book so far mean to our children?

How accepting should we the parents at present be on our children getting involved with technology? These types of questions deal with different approaches in the western world, but how about Bangladesh? If parents tell their children not to use Facebook, it will simply impact on their personal relationship and on the other side of the spectrum, it is difficult for parents to know what their children are actually doing with social media.

Are they preparing themselves for mobile marketing in Bangladesh? Are they spawning themselves to be productive through deep conversations on Facebook? Probably not.

It is thus important to initiate discussion with our children who are the leaders of the future Bangladesh to make them understand what values they get and what disadvantages out there while they are using technology.

That is how the difficult challenges, new media brings can be handled for the future generations. We need to work together in protecting the future right of media usage and access for the coming generation in Bangladesh parallel to other nations in the world.

I in this book have tried to represent a picture of what is at stake in the electronic media world in Bangladesh. Now it is our duty to prove that the initiatives taken by me here can be ratcheted up for ongoing electronic media development in Bangladesh by putting required resources and effort into it.

CONCLUSION

" Nothing is more dangerous than an idea, when it's the
only one we have. "

-Émile Chartier-

In spring 2008 I went to Italy for the first time. I realized
Italians do not live to work instead they work to live and
that they value art. I heard a story of Michelangelo there and
I am referring that from Rolf Dobelli's bestselling "The Art of
Thinking Clearly"[1]. The story goes like this: when the Pope
asked Michelangelo what was his secret of being such a genius
and how he has created the statue of David-the masterpiece of
all masterpieces, Michelangelo replied that it was very simple, all
he did was removed everything that was not David.

I wish I could know for sure what I needed to remove from
this book to honestly recognize the answer of the question that
was modelled by this book at the beginning, "What's Happening
to Our TV?".

I however, tried to remove everything that is not happening
to our TV and that way tried to reflect on what is actually
happening to our TV now. The foundations for searching an
answer for the question posed by the title of this book were then
structured by individual aspects discussed in the five Chapters.

However, the discussions of the different Chapters below should be read by generalizing different aspects, that is to say, they can be interpreted in general electronic media development perspective and not only from the context of Bangladesh electronic media.

The ability of the audience to control the success of media organization remains a contentious methodological issue as we have seen in the first Chapter. I believe it is difficult for us to generalize what the audience likes since it is situational and we must learn from the different associated challenges.

Our media industries would produce healthier content if more audiences took part in content generation. In this respect a concept titled open audience-innovation was introduced by me. We should try to get the most out of the audiences and prevent bias.

Understanding the market, based on the requirement and competence of the modern audiences is also crucial and the concept of niche marketing was introduced and discussed regarding this. However, it is important to ensure that the professionals do it in a challenging and fun way and show the different concepts in practice rather than discussions only.

The discussions in Chapter 2 illustrated the range of factors that can drive audience perception and impact in the direction of improved content generation. Pervasive nature of persuasion can be a useful approach to realizing the perception in a novel way. Realizing the characteristics and strengths of media psychology in this respect is thus the fundamental thing.

Understanding of persuasive design in the media content generation would then take a different shift where new usable cognitive models can be derived toward the success of content design and improved audience understanding.

One of such cognitive model was derived and discussed in this Chapter as an example. If we want to build successful media content we must think intuitively and explore the market from a psychological point of view which is why the concept of cognitive market was discussed within the context of media development.

Media professionals should ensure that these pervasive natures of different psychological issues as discussed in Chapter 2 are practiced in their organizations for giving content development and audience understanding a solid good start.

Realizing what "understanding" truly means in audience analysis and their perception of media, can be used to improve the content beyond the scopes of modern and traditional audiences and this was the conclusion of Chapter 3.

Different issues related to content at present and their remedies were discussed to show how new business scopes and competition in the market can be triggered in the electronic media business and why they are important to consider in the planning phase of content generation. A sample design space in the form of a framework illustrated the process of content creation from a new perspective while advance discussions on how to handle different process and method for optimal content generation and then take care different associated risks with content were given a special focus.

Digital media economics is not only a very promising concept to secure financial position for media organizations, but it also together with improved business model and guidelines can be used for organizational improvements. This concept was elaborated in Chapter 4 with the help of some key areas of reform like the potential of internet towards the shift of economic success for profitability and financial stability of the media organizations.

Management must address these areas simultaneously if the company is to overcome its present poor record. However, it must be remembered that this analysis is quite limited and a depth understanding and evaluation can occur during the utilization of the concepts discussed in this Chapter.

At present, the media organizations in Bangladesh do not show strong prospects in the areas of profitability, liquidity or stability in relation to their audience and content that they produce, and therefore they should be concerned with these issues as discussed in Chapter 3 for initiating a better return on the investment process.

In the end, a clear distinction between what is happening to our TV and where we are heading was identified while discussing a digital social revolution that has already partially risen in Bangladesh. While the scope of using social media is enormous for triggering this revolution, political paradigm in Bangladesh can be a drawback against it.

Public awareness and change of attitude for the policy makers were indicated to be some of the underlying challenges that the future generations of Bangladesh need to focus on. However, it is important to be prepared for adapting the changes that technologies bring into our life and deal with the other additional issues like politics or policy making.

Otherwise, Bangladesh media industry will be facing tough challenges in the future and the audience departure from local TV channels will continue to occur at a rate faster than it is happening now. Such consequences for sure will not be very pleasing at all, for strengthening the social and cultural images of Bangladesh in the international market.

When I started writing this book I did not think that the book will end up creating any process. But if you join lines between the Chapters you notice that an iterative process has been shaped by the substances from this book. From understanding the modern audiences towards their pervasive psychological interpretation of improved content generation intended for stable and productive position creation in competitive markets and thereby acting towards a successful social revolution in Bangladesh ultimately again takes us back into sharing the audience thought phase.

We interpret different thoughts from the digital social revolution as an outcome of a process and then use those views to improve methodologies in audience analysis in turn. Thus, the book has, not deliberately created an iterative process that I can entitle to be a process for electronic media research and development in Bangladesh.

So what exactly is happening to our TV in Bangladesh that we can conclude after discovering the present trends and beyond? Like my old friends and relatives, we cannot say anymore that nothing is happening with our TV, as I pointed out in the introduction section. We see that there are a lot of things going on with our electronic media and a lot are going to happen to our TV in the near and coming future.

At present, it seems what is happening to our TV is that the policy makers together with the media professionals are playing safe within an incomplete scope, probably because they are too afraid of escaping from their safety boundary. This is why we are falling behind with other potentials, our audiences are misplacing their interest on other out of the country TV channels and this is why the hardest bureaucratic dilemma works in a never ending loophole for triggering personal gain instead of holistic development of the media industries in Bangladesh.

I hope this book pushes us to rethink these issues when Bangladesh is going through the most powerful buildup phase than ever before for fostering success in different sectors.

We are living in a world that is filled with strange problems, but we also have creative opportunities to solve them. But to do this requires different ideas and thoughts that are unique. Efficiency and cost-effectiveness are not enough anymore to be competitive in today's comprehensive market.

What matters now is to make the creative ideas happen for solving problems and establish it. So can we think like this to inspire fresh ideas? Can we build organizations that can inspire us? Maxwell[3] quoted management trainer Sir Antony Jay, "The uncreative mind can spot wrong answers, but it takes a creative mind to spot wrong questions" to point out the importance of identifying wrong questions since they discontinue the possibility for improved thinking for any development.

Fresh idea generation is thus not an accidental event[2], neither it is any magic; rather it needs a transformation of vision to the reality. This book was a small effort from me to inspire you who might be the leading media professionals in future Bangladesh and are curious to understand the situation of present electronic media to follow the trends for future development by pointing out some right questions.

It is not like that the individual Chapters of this book will inspire you from the foundation of each Chapter, rather it probably can help by inspiring you towards the facts that you like to do which apparently will work towards the purpose of this book. But then again, as Belsky[2] suggested, just having an idea is the small part of the process and in this respect quoted Thomas Edison's famous joke, "Genius is 1 percent inspiration and 99 percent perspiration." My job in this book was this 1 percent inspiration and it is in your hand to make the rest of the 99 percent to happen.

References

INTRODUCTION

1. Arden, P. (2003). It's not how good you are, it's how good you want to be. Phaidon.

2. Petroski, H. (2006). Success through failure: The paradox of design. Princeton University Press.

3. Maxwell, J. C. (2009). How successful people think: Change your thinking, change your life. Hachette UK.

4. Sinek, S. (2011). Start with why: How great leaders inspire everyone to take action. Penguin UK.

5. Belsky, S. (2012). Making ideas happen: Overcoming the obstacles between vision and reality. Penguin UK.

CHAPTER 1: THE NEW AUDIENCES

1. Livingstone, S. (2004). The challenge of changing audiences or, what is the audience researcher to do in the age of the Internet?. European journal of communication, 19(1), 75-86.

2. Livingstone, S. (1998). Audience research at the crossroads The'implied audience'in media and cultural theory. European journal of cultural studies, 1(2), 193-217.

3. Chesbrough, H. W. (2006). Open innovation: The new imperative for creating and profiting from technology. Harvard Business Press.

4. Mustaquim, M. M., & Nyström, T. (2014, September). Open Sustainability Innovation—A Pragmatic Standpoint of Sustainable HCI. In International Conference on Business Informatics Research (pp. 101-112). Springer International Publishing.

5. Dalgic, T., & Leeuw, M. (1994). Niche marketing revisited: concept, applications, and some European cases. European Journal of Marketing, 28(4), 39-55.

6. Sarrina Li, S. C. (2001). New media and market competition: A niche analysis of television news, electronic news, and newspaper news in Taiwan. Journal of Broadcasting & Electronic Media, 45(2), 259-276.

7. Kovach, B., & Rosenstiel, T. (2007). The elements of journalism: What newspeople should know and the public should expect. Three Rivers Press (CA).

8. Lupia, A., & McCubbins, M. D. (1998). The democratic dilemma: Can citizens learn what they need to know?. Cambridge University Press.

CHAPTER 2: PERVASIVE PERSUASION

1. Rutledge, P. (2010). What is Media Psychology? And Why You Should Care. Media Psychology Research Center.

2. Fogg, B.J. (2009). A Behavior Model for Persuasive Design, Proceeding of the 4th International Conference on Persuasive Technology, Persuasive'09, Claremont, CA, United States, ACM International Conference Proceeding Series 2009.

3. Fogg, B.J., (2003). Persuasive technology: Using computers

to change what we think and do. Morgan Kaufmann Publishers, San Francisco

4. Fogg, B.J., Nass, C., (1997). How Users Reciprocate to Computers: An experiment that demonstrates behavior change, In Proceedings of CHI 1997, ACM Press, 331-332.

5. Mustaquim, M. and Nyström, T. 2014. Designing Persuasive Systems for Sustainability – A Cognitive Dissonance Model. In Proceedings of the European Conference on Information Systems (ECIS) 2014, Tel Aviv, Israel, June 9-11, 2014.

6. Shallice, T. (1988). From neuropsychology to mental structure. Cambridge University Press.

7. White, J. C., Varadarajan, P. R., & Dacin, P. A. (2003). Market situation interpretation and response: The role of cognitive style, organizational culture, and information use. Journal of Marketing, 67(3), 63-79.

8. Kovach, B., & Rosenstiel, T. (2007). The elements of journalism: What newspeople should know and the public should expect. Three Rivers Press (CA).

CHAPTER 3: CONTENT EVOLUATION

1. Van Koert, R. (2000). Providing content and facilitating social change: Electronic media in rural development based on case material from Peru. First Monday, 5(2).

2. Van Tassel, J. (2012). Managing Electronic Media: Making, Moving and Marketing Digital Content. CRC Press.

3. Kahneman, D. (2011). Thinking, fast and slow. Macmillan.

4. Taleb, N. N. (2007). The black swan: The impact of the highly improbable. Random house.

5. Saleem, M., & Anderson, C. A. (2012). The good, the bad, and the ugly of electronic media. Applying social science to reduce violent offending, 83-101.

6. WEF. (2016). The Impact of Digital Content: Opportunities and Risks of Creating and Sharing Information Online *World Economic Forum, Geneva.*

7. Mustaquim, M. M., & Nyström, T. (2015, May). Information System Design Space for Sustainability. In International Conference on Design Science Research in Information Systems (pp. 39-54). Springer International Publishing.

CHAPTER 4: ECONOMIC EXTENSION

1. WEF. (2016). How does digital media really affect us? *World Economic Forum, Geneva.*

2. Puddephatt, A. (2010). Sida's guidelines for media development. Stockholm: Swedish International Development Agency.

3. Alexander, A., Owers, J. E., Carveth, R., Hollifield, C. A., & Greco, A. N. (Eds.). (2003). Media economics: Theory and practice. Routledge.

4. Collins, R., Garnham, N., & Locksley, G. (1988). The economics of television: The UK case. Newbury Park, CA: Sage

5. Manyika, J., & Roxburgh, C. (2011). The great transformer:

The impact of the Internet on economic growth and prosperity. McKinsey Global Institute, 1.

6. Leminen, S., Salo, J., Helle, M., Huhtala, J. P., Kivikangas, M., Penttinen, E., ... & Tölö, M. (2010). eReading Services, Business Models and Concepts in Media Industry.

7. Osterwalder, A., & Pigneur, Y. (2010). Business model generation: a handbook for visionaries, game changers, and challengers. John Wiley & Sons.

CHAPTER 5: DIGITAL SOCIAL REVOLUTION

1. WEF. (2015). Are you ready for the technological revolution? World Economic Forum, Geneva.

2. John V. Pavlik, citing James Beniger, New Media Technology: Cultural and Commercial Perspectives, 2nd ed. (Boston: Allyn and Bacon, 1998), 134.

3. Kraidy, M. M. (2002). Globalization of culture through the media. Encyclopedia of communication and information, 359.

4. Boas, T., Dunning, T., & Bussell, J. (2005). Will the digital revolution revolutionize development? Drawing together the debate. Studies in Comparative International Development, 40(2), 95-110.

5. Flew, T., Spurgeon, C., Daniel, A., & Swift, A. (2012). The promise of computational journalism. Journalism Practice, 6(2), 157-171.

CONCLUSIONS

1. Dobelli, R. (2015). The Art of Thinking Clearly-Edisi Bahasa

Melayu. PTS Publications & Distributors Sdn Bhd.

2. Belsky, S. (2012). Making ideas happen: Overcoming the obstacles between vision and reality. Penguin UK.

3. Maxwell, J. C. (2009). How successful people think: Change your thinking, change your life. Hachette UK.

About the Author

Having worked in the electronic media industry for the last sixteen years, Samia Rahman has fostered the leading media organizations along with the first terrestrial private TV channel in Bangladesh. Samia has written five books on the topic of electronic media available in the Bengali language. As well, she has been a popular columnist, book editor and critical political analyst who also published over a dozen scientific research articles. She is recognized as one of the top media personality in Bangladesh and is the head of current affairs in a private TV channel. Samia is a two-times gold medal winner from the University of Dhaka, Faculty of Mass Communication and Journalism, where she works as an Associate Professor.

You can visit her at www.samiarahman.com